THE
CORPORATE
SCRIPTWRITING
BOOK

A Step-by-Step Guide to Writing
Business Films, Videotapes & Slide Shows

THE CORPORATE SCRIPTWRITING BOOK

A Step-by-Step Guide to Writing Business Films, Videotapes & Slide Shows

by DONNA MATRAZZO

Cover by Kathleen Reilly
Illustrations by Joe Kowal

COMMUNICOM PUBLISHING COMPANY
Publishers/Portland

To Bob Passaro,
who believed in me.

THE CORPORATE SCRIPTWRITING BOOK

Library of Congress Catalog Card Number: 80-81823

ISBN: 0-932617-07-7
(previously published by Media Concepts Press
under ISBN 0-935608-01-X)

First printing, July, 1980
Second printing, September, 1981
Third printing, July, 1982
Fourth printing (revised), January, 1985

Contents

Preface

You have an assignment: to write a script. It may be for a corporation, a hospital, a school, a government agency, or any other sort of organization. What are you supposed to do? Where do you begin? What do you do next? What do other people expect of you? How can you tell if your script is good?

When I took on my first such assignment, I, quite frankly, didn't know. And I didn't know anyone to ask. When I finally found some people to answer some things, I discovered that there was no single place to find all I needed to know to do my job well.

So, I learned the roundabout way, but I did find answers. I learned by trial and error, by talking with other writers, by reading everything about scriptwriting I could find, and by DOING, day in and day out, for years. This book shares those discoveries.

This book is not going to guarantee that you will produce magnificent scripts. That must come from you, from your talents, your dedication and your hard work.

What this book **will** do is save you perhaps a year or two of roundabout learning, so that you can produce better scripts, sooner. It will teach you the basics, so that they can become second nature, and you can move on to develop your writing skills.

This book will tell you the whys, hows and wherefores of bringing a script into existence. And it will show you how to proceed as a professional, so that you can feel confident of yourself and your work.

A good script does not happen by a writer sitting down to write. That is the last thing a writer does, after a great deal of preparation, research and design. This book will explore all those stages.

This book is the beginning.

Acknowledgements

Many thanks to all the writers
who have shared their expertise
with me.

Special thanks, for their inspiration
and help with this manuscript, to Jody
Smith, James Ambandos, Marijane
Cardell, John Foerster, Ed Harding
and Kathleen Reilly.

1
Off-Screen Credits

The Scene: a Party, any Party.

> "What do you do for a living?"
>
> "I'm a writer."
>
> "A writer! How glamorous! What do you write? Let me guess . . . romance novels . . . I can see it in your eyes . . ."
>
> "I'm a scriptwriter."
>
> "A **script**writer! I should have known. Byron, come over here and meet this young lady . . . She's a scriptwriter. This is so exciting! What films have you written? Or is it TV?"
>
> "I write industrial films."
>
> "Oh. Um, well, yes . . . If you'll excuse me, I think I'm ready for another drink. Nice talking to you, dear."

Business films. Video sales presentations. Slide training programs. Corporate TV news. Somehow, they never sound very glamorous. Glamorous, they're not,

1

perhaps, but they certainly **are** exciting, challenging, creative, and very rewarding.

"Business films" is a drab moniker; a better phrase might be: creative, purposeful audio visual presentations.

Your work is creative because you learn all about a subject, condense that information, and design a unique, enjoyable experience from it. Then you translate that design into a script which can be produced in a short time on a shoestring budget. Ingenious work, indeed.

What you write is purposeful because your shows make things happen. Just days, weeks or months after the pages come out of your typewriter, your shows are out there teaching, communicating, informing, motivating, or selling. A fulfilling business, for sure.

Myriad Advantages

This field presents a great many opportunities you won't find anywhere else.

For example, because shows are non-broadcast (not shown over broadcast television or in theatres), you have much creative freedom. Anyone writing TV commercials will tell you how every word of copy, even insinuations, must endure an endless barrage of legal and client scrutiny. Within most organizations, you are given greater liberties.

You have an enormous amount of control over your creative concepts and the final show. Hollywood screenwriters rarely expect to see the finished films look precisely like their scripts. Most of the time, you can.

Where other writers must draw from their own experiences or spend months or years researching a theme, you will have one presented to you.

You learn something new all the time. You learn it thoroughly, and you learn it from the experts, often world-renowned experts.

You work near your audiences, so you can go to the place where your show is played, watch an audience and gauge how well you've done.

Because you are part of an organization, your work becomes something much bigger than your own aspirations. You develop a sense of pride in your organization and its work, and you help contribute to its success.

You derive a great sense of accomplishment. You move people, teach them, inform them, convince them, or expand their awareness. That's something very real and very immediate. And that's all very exciting.

An Abundance of Rewards

The rewards are as varied as there are writers and assignments. Some might be:

The satisfaction of understanding atomic absorption spectrophotometry so well that you have simplified it for a high school audience.

The discovery that a newly-hired deaf woman couldn't learn how to operate a computer CRT terminal until she saw (yet couldn't even hear!) your show.

The knowledge that your work is helping to sell educational products used to teach children in Third World countries.

The receipt of hundreds of letters of thanks from people who saw your program on safety, with comments that they are adopting the prescribed methods.

A memo that your company's Board of Directors received a letter from their stock brokers saying, "The film was a big hit, as it gave a clear understanding of the company. It also provided the investment community with confidence that your company is interested in presenting the whole picture."

A phone call from a sales representative who used your show to break a $900,000 account. He said, "That videotape is the most powerful product selling tool ever developed. It sure made our job easier."

A report from one client who introduced your film to the sales people who would use it. He remarked, "They were extremely proud and thought it outstanding. We plan to show it throughout the world."

The winning of an award, which was presented by and even brought a kiss from your favorite TV anchorperson.

Sometimes, too, there is a touch of real glamor. People have had the chance to work with, among others, E.G. Marshall, Katharine Ross, Cliff Robertson, Lloyd Bridges, Robin "Mork" Williams and even The Muppets.

Whatever rewards you find, your scriptwriting will undoubtedly offer some unique opportunities and remarkable experiences.

2
The Roles of the Scriptwriter

You have a script to write, so you've officially become a scriptwriter. What, exactly, are you supposed to do? To write the script, of course, but that's only part of it.

The scriptwriter for an organization is, in a way, an anomaly. You must be imaginative, yet be tempered with a sophisticated business sense. You must be outgoing and able to work within a team, yet must do your own serious work in solitude. You must be independent, ready to take the initiative, yet able to make compromises.

You have many roles to fill, arising from the nature of the scriptwriter's many responsibilities. These will differ from job to job and assignment to assignment, but there are some basic things that are expected of the writer:

1. You will plan and conduct an initial interview or meeting, sometimes called THE

PRE-SCRIPT MEETING, to begin getting information about the project.

2. You will carry out all the necessary RESEARCH, including interviews.

3. You will write a TREATMENT or an outline, and get your client to approve it.

4. Naturally, you will write the SCRIPT, usually a Rough Draft revised into a Shooting Script.

5. You, and only you, will have to PRESENT, or sell, the script.

Skills and Talents

As the scriptwriter, you must be a Public Relations specialist. You will be on your own, representing yourself, a department, and perhaps an entire company, to clients and other people.

You should be a curious, intelligent and enthusiastic researcher, finding opportunities where others despair.

You ought to be well-organized at all times.

As the scriptwriter, you must be knowledgeable about production. You must know the capabilities and limitations of the equipment, people and budgets available to you.

You must be an imaginative and talented concept creator; at times, you're going to have to work wonders with some mighty dull subjects.

You will have to become a skillful and dedicated scriptwriter. You must know how to write for the screen, and how to hide away with a typewriter until each show is as good as you can make it.

Finally, you must be a good presenter and salesperson. If you can't "sell" your script to the client, it won't ever be produced.

From Public Relations Specialist, to Researcher, to Organizer, to Producer, to Writer, to Salesperson. Is that too much to expect?

Like most writers, you probably feel weak in some areas and strong in others. But you must have a little of each of these skills. It doesn't help to be great at digging out information if you leave your notes where a pet gerbil can eat them. And, you can write the most wonderful script in the world, but your client will never believe that if you present it with a dour face.

Through the following pages, you ought to become enlightened, or frightened, into caring about each of these matters.

3
From Author
to Scriptwriter

Most scriptwriters in our field, if they have a background in writing at all, have been print writers. They've come from journalism, public relations, training, advertising, corporate communications and a variety of other fields.

This may change in the near future, with many colleges offering courses in scriptwriting, but today few scriptwriters in organizations have begun their careers as such.

What happens as you go from author to scriptwriter? To begin with, you must recognize that writing isn't writing isn't writing. You are entering a very different realm. You wouldn't expect to make an easy transition between writing technical manuals and writing poetry, and the same is true here.

The Page vs the Screen

In the first place, a script is never an end in itself, as is the printed page. The audience for your show will never see your script. What you write is merely a design, with technical prescriptions, for a visual and auditory message which, unless you are also the director, someone else will create.

Perhaps the script can be compared to sheet music. Do music-lovers sit down and "ooh" and "ahh" over sheet music? No, they appreciate the performance of that music, which is a musician's transformation and interpretation of the composer's work.

A script is something like that. The finished program, or performance, is your work, and then again it isn't. It has become something else.

A script is not a literary endeavor. As an author, you expect your words to carry your message. In an audio visual production, the spoken words (those which the audience hears) do the least of the message-carrying.

Your message comes across most strongly by the visuals, in conjunction with music and sound effects. Actually, the spoken words are the least memorable.

This may sound preposterous, but a number of research studies have shown that people learn most from and remember what they **see.** Their feelings and vivid recollections are of scenes and non-verbal messages, like posture and intonation. Amazingly enough, people remember very, very little of the words they hear.

There is an old Chinese proverb which begins, "I hear and I forget. I see and I remember." That could be a philosophy behind audio visual programs.

What does this mean for you? This means that you don't become a scriptwriter by simply using a script format. You must **think** visually. You must find ways to impart your information and the message you create from it through what will be seen.

Descriptions are no longer adjectives. They are scenes and props. For example, it's quite a simple matter to say in print, "the imposter, posing as a bank guard." In a script, you must show that the person **is** an imposter. The man's donning a uniform doesn't tell the audience that it doesn't belong to him. You will have to establish the person as something else, and show that the bank guard's uniform is not his.

Time is another complex matter. "Three years ago" is easier to write than to show. How do you let your audience know that it's early morning, March, or the year 1550 without resorting to cliché clocks and calendars?

From Other Angles

Another major difference in scriptwriting is the audience. You have two kinds of audiences. The first are the "captives". These people may be shown your production as part of a group at work, in a classroom at school, in a hospital bed, or in the middle of a sales call. They are, in a sense, captive because they can't just get up and walk away.

The second kind of audience, the "independents", can. They may be insurance agents, car dealers, teachers, or others who receive a copy of your program and have the option of squeezing a viewing into a very busy day. If they do decide to watch it, they can turn it off and walk away the instant they feel like it.

Both of these audiences can, and will, turn off their minds.

This gives you a different responsibility as a writer. You must be communicating with the audience at all times. You must get to know and understand the people in your audience. You must learn what they know and how they feel about this topic, so that you can present your information in a way that will grab and hold their attention.

In your concern for the audience, you must make all scenes self-evident. If you throw in a word people won't understand or a scene that doesn't fit, you've taken the audience down a side road. You've lost them. Maybe it's only for a few seconds or a minute, but during that time you were showing them something else and they missed that, too.

If you do this too often, you may lose the audience for good. Remember, the viewer can't consult a dictionary and may not be able to go back over a scene again and again to understand what took place.

The Author's Resources

All in all, the change from author to scriptwriter is extremely difficult. If you approach it that way, it's more likely that you'll do well.

On the heartening side, you should realize that you already have a great many of the necessary skills and assets.

For one thing, a scriptwriter in this field is an information writer, as opposed to an entertainment writer. True, shows should be entertaining and enjoyable, but except in a few special cases, the entertainment factor is not foremost. You are an information writer already.

You know, probably quite well, how to conduct research, how to interview people, and how to weed through and organize vast amounts of material to communicate information. In our field, that is at least half of the work. So, you're halfway there.

The best part is, that's the tough half. What you must learn to do now, to think and write in visuals and sounds, is great fun. You've grown up with television and film; now you must simply become more aware of how to use them to communicate your message.

You have other advantages, too. Because you have worked in a corporate or organizational environment, you have developed a sense of sophisticated business communications. You know better than to write something that's delightful but useless; you have a sense of the realities of business. You understand that there's room for creativity, but that it must evolve from the information you want to impart, instead of the other way around.

And you know that the essence of your craft is solving problems for your company or organization.

What you will do as a scriptwriter is translate those hard-earned skills into another medium. Your goal, then, is to become a superb scriptwriter. It won't be easy, guaranteed! But it most assuredly will be a rewarding adventure.

4
The Script as Blueprint

Why have a script at all? Many people think all that's needed to produce a good show is a strong idea, a general plan, and a few scribbled notes. Sure, a show can be produced that way. But will there be any guarantee that it will turn out as planned? A script is that guarantee, of sorts.

The script for a show can be paralleled to the blueprints for a house. If you were planning to build a house, how would you proceed? Would you begin with a general idea and a plot of land, then head out there carrying a hammer, nails and two-by-fours? Without a blueprint, would you simply start building that house?

Yet that is just what many people do to produce audio visual programs. They begin with a rough plan, then they head out to the location with sketchy notes, a crew and equipment.

In both cases, you have the same problems. It's almost impossible to get the finished product to reflect your imagined one. It's likely that the parts won't fit together, because you hadn't figured out if they would. Then what happens? You have to improvise. So the finished product costs more and is even further removed from the idea you first envisioned.

A blueprint is a thorough, step-by-step representation on paper of exactly what the finished product will be like, with explicit directions of all that's needed to put it together.

A script is that, too. It is a thorough, step-by-step representation on paper of exactly what the finished product will be like, with explicit directions of all that's needed to put it together.

Blueprints and scripts are working documents. They are designs for materials needed and steps to be taken. Their value and artistic merit come not from the writing and drawing, but from how well those elements function as representatives of the finished product.

In this sense, a script is not even as good a representation as a blueprint. A blueprint uses lines and spaces to depict lines and spaces. A script must use **words** to describe pictures and sounds.

A Script Creates a Structure

What does happen with a good script?

The script serves as a catalyst for communication among the writer, client and production team. Everyone will know what to expect from the finished show, and what is expected of each of them. It helps to eliminate misunderstanding and confusion.

A script means that you know your ideas will work. By writing every element of a script explicitly, scene for scene, location for location, actor for actor, prop for prop, special effect for special effect and word for word, you force yourself to think through every outrageous idea and bring it to producible terms. If you can't make an idea work in your script, you must throw it out.

A good script saves money. The producer knows, and shoots, only what is needed. The unproducible ideas have been recognized and discarded on paper, not on location, where the producer is ringing up hundreds, maybe thousands, of dollars a day in crew, equipment and travel expenses.

A script gives all the people involved all the information they need to budget, plan, coordinate and shoot the entire program.

A good script is an inspiration. The client will become excited about the show and will assure complete cooperation, often far above and beyond what anyone expected. The production people become anxious to begin with their "hammers and nails" because they know they're involved in a project of which they're going to be proud.

Most of all, a good script is as close as anyone can come to a guarantee that a show can, and will, work.

5
The Pre-Script Meeting

Where does a script begin? For the writer, it begins with the script assignment. (It is assumed that someone has already done the work of deciding that a videotape, film or slide show is needed.)

The writer's first job is to find out as much information as possible about the intended program and its purpose. The best way to do that is to schedule a Pre-Script Meeting with the client.

Who is the client? The client is the person who requested the show and will pay for it. It could be anyone inside or related to your organization, maybe a department head, a marketing manager, or a senior vice president.

In most cases, the Pre-Script Meeting will be your first face-to-face encounter with this client. This person's first impression of you is of the utmost importance. You must create an aura of professionalism which will inspire the client's confidence in you. More than that, the client must

feel so comfortable about you that he or she would not hesitate to send you to interview the company president.

This client who has never met you before, or possibly never worked with a scriptwriter before, is bound to have mixed feelings about you.

On the one hand, clients are very excited about creating a show about their special product or topic. But on the other hand, clients are wary of this "creative person". What you do is very mysterious, and they are committing a chunk of their budgets to what seems to them a figment of your wild imagination.

Getting Ready

You can alleviate some of that uncertainty and make what you're doing seem more "factual" by a few business-like maneuvers.

Before the meeting, send the client a memo, re-iterating the date, time and place. Mention the things you will need to know and need to do. For example, you will probably want to take a tour of the facilities or meet specific people. Ask the client to gather any reference material that you can bring back with you.

If you know something about the proposed show, i.e., that it will be Quarterly Report or a Plant Tour, and you've done a program that's similar, you might want to send it along as a sample. The client will get a feeling for what he or she likes and doesn't like about the show, and will see what you can do.

The day before the meeting, prepare a list of questions, or use a Program Planner.

Read through any material the client may have already sent. Gather your materials: tablet, pens, tape recorder, perhaps a sample tape or script. Will you need a camera? Plane tickets? Expense money? Anything else?

Get a good night's sleep; you're going to have to absorb a lot the next day. And prepare to look nice and business-like. In most instances, you'll be meeting with people who are dressed conservatively in suits. You'll feel more comfortable if you do likewise.

If you cringe at the thought of three-piece suits and such, take heart in the theory of country-western singer Dolly Parton. Despite her outlandish hair and clothes, she insists that she's just a farm girl who understands that there's a magic in looking one way while being just the opposite inside.

And be practical. If it's likely that you'll be going on a tour of a truck manufacturing plant, don't wear your lightest-color suit.

Program Planner, Side 1

Date _____   Meeting with _____
Requested by _____   Name, Title _____
_____   Phone _____

WHAT IS THIS SHOW EXPECTED TO DO? (PROBLEM/SOLUTION)

PURPOSE: □ To inform   □ To teach   □ To sell   □ To motivate   □ Other

Is this show part of a series? Explain.

Of what value will this program be to your business?

Obstacles?

AUDIENCE

Occupation
Men/Women, Age
Present Knowledge of Topic
Present Attitude Toward Topic

AFTER VIEWING THE TAPE, WHAT SHOULD THE VIEWER ...

Know?

Think?

Feel?

Do?

PRODUCTION SPECIFICATIONS

Producer
Director
Production Facility
Budget

SCHEDULE
Treatment Due
Rough Script Due
Final Script Due
Possible Shooting Dates
Finished Program Needed

CONTENT ELEMENTS

Program Planner, Side 2

TECHNICAL ADVISOR(S)

Name
Title
Phone

OTHER SOURCES OF INFORMATION

PRINTED MATERIALS

Ready now?

Where to find?

LOCATIONS TO VISIT/TOUR

Contact: Name, Title
           Phone

Make arrangements now?

PRESENTATION FORMAT

Size of screen

Number of people in audience:

Length specifications?

Discussion Leader?

Support Materials?

Means for Feedback/Evaluation?

PERSON WITH THE FINAL SAY

LEGAL DEPARTMENT APPROVAL?

Other approvals?

ANYTHING ELSE?

The Meeting

Your first concern at this meeting is to find out the client's problem. Problem? How do you know that the client has a problem?

The only reason for doing any production is that the client has a problem that your show is expected to solve. Before you go any further, you have to IDENTIFY THE PROBLEM. You ask, "What is this show expected to do?" The solution to the problem leads you to your show's purpose.

For example, a client's problem might be, "We aren't selling enough chemicals and it's because people don't believe we **make** the stuff. They think we just re-package it." So, the solution to the problem might be, "To show the R&D and the manufacturing process to prove we manufacture the product."

Use that solution to DECIDE ON THE SHOW'S PURPOSE. In this case, the purpose might be, "To sell chemicals by showing the care and quality which go into the R&D and manufacturing process." What is the show expected to do? It's to sell chemicals.

You should always try to narrow the goals down to **one** purpose: to inform, to teach, to sell, to motivate, and so forth.

Now is a good time to ask if this show is part of a series. If it is, some of the following questions may already be answered for you.

You should ask of what value this show will be to the client's business. A line of products may be resting on the success of this show and it's important for you to realize this.

And you should also ask if there are any obstacles this show must overcome, like the fact that your chemicals are the most expensive on the market.

Next, you must DETERMINE THE AUDIENCE. Find out who will see the show. Are they mostly men? Women? What are their occupations? What do they already know and how do they feel about the topic? This is very critical. You can't expect to hold the audience's interest if you're telling them things they already know or talking over their heads. You may find out you must battle preconceived notions or negative attitudes.

We have the advantage of getting to know about the people in our audiences and why they're watching our shows. Try and find out from the client as much as you can about these people.

Then find out what effects your client wants this show to have on the audience. What should they KNOW? That you manufacture chemicals. What should they THINK? That these chemicals are of high quality, worth paying extra for. What should they FEEL? That such high quality chemicals would improve the performance of their instruments. What should they DO? Buy your chemicals.

So, at this meeting, you must find out as much as possible about the people in this audience, and where to find out more. All of this is just the beginning.

At this meeting, you must also learn:

Production Specifications. Usually, the other people working on this show, the production facility and the budget will be determined beforehand. Here, you confirm them.

The Deadlines. If possible, you should decide upon a schedule for the Rough and Final Scripts, and possible shooting dates. Definitely find out the date for intended distribution of the finished production.

The Content. The client will probably have in mind a number of areas which must be included. In the case of a script about chemical manufacturing, for example, the client may want a history of the Chemical Division, a tour of the plant and a demonstration of packaging containers.

Technical Advisor(s). Someone called a Technical Advisor or Subject Matter Expert should be appointed to be responsible for the technical accuracy of the script and the production. Find out who this person will be and where he or she can be reached.

Major Sources of Information. Find out names and phone numbers of resource people and collect printed material.

Locations to Visit. There are places you may tour that day, and other places the client may suggest you visit. It's a good idea if the client makes those arrangements for you, since he or she is familiar with the people in charge of those places and by calling, gives endorsement to your visit.

Finished Format and Means of Distribution. How will the audience see your show? Find out the kind of equipment and screen, the size of screen, size of room, number of people who will watch together, whether it will be on company time, and so forth. Will the showing be part of a discussion group? Will there be support material? A means for feedback and evaluation? These things will influence your approach to the show.

The Availability of Client and Others. You should find out if the client will be out of town, if the Operations Manager or other resource person will take a vacation soon, and so forth. Ask for business cards from people you're likely to have to call.

The Person with the Final Say. Find out who will actually have the final say, which may or may not be the client. Also find out if there are other people who will have to approve your script.

Any Pre-Determined Ideas or Limitations. Maybe someone has already decided that the client or a vice president **will** be the host or hostess of this show. Or maybe the client has an idea for the Treatment.

What happens, you ask, if you are adamantly opposed to the client's idea? First of all, try not to show it. One writer says you should answer "Marvelous! Now let me be sure I have that all down ..." and later come back with your own ideas.

In essence, this is true. Listen and be interested, especially to **why** the client thinks this will work. If you have genuine, objective concerns, perhaps regarding the budget or finding an actor to play such a part, express them now.

The fact of the matter is, there is a chance that you may have to use the client's idea. It may be a matter of ego. It may be a matter of politics. It may be that you won't be able to come up with an idea which you can convince your client is better. (Yes, this happens!)

In general, if you dislike a client's ideas, the best solution is to bite your tongue, smile, then plan to go home and work like crazy. Usually, you do come up with a better idea (or some adaptation of the client's), you present it with your reasons, and the client loves it!

Once you have covered all these areas with the client and your meeting is over, you will probably be taken on a tour of the facility, given printed material and introduced to some of the people who will eventually be involved in the production.

Later that day, if you didn't use a tape recorder, review your notes and fill them in while everything is still fresh in your mind. Sometimes other projects come up and you may not have the chance to work on this script right away.

After you've asked all of those questions of other people, you'll find that you now have a few for yourself: "How will I ever get all this done in time?" and "Where do I begin?"

6
The Key to the Script: The Audience

The key to your script is your audience. You should begin work on your show by giving some thought to these people because, from this point on, everything you do must be done with them in mind.

A lot of people will tell you that this audience doesn't expect a Hollywood production from an in-house audio visual department. Don't fool yourself. You do indeed have a sophisticated audience. That doesn't mean just the corporate executives and PhD's. That goes for everyone.

Everyone who watches your show is somewhat of an expert on television and film. After all, for years they've been watching the tube and going to the movies. Everyone's a critic; can you really believe that they won't be critical of your show?

This audience is accustomed to high quality, well-paced and well-produced programs. It doesn't matter what kind of cameras you have, and it doesn't matter that you can't afford Walter

Cronkite to do your company news. If your show isn't good, the audience won't pay attention. If you are boring, have content inconsistencies or obvious technical problems, the audience will immediately recognize it.

Besides being screen-sophisticates, your audience has another important feature: their state of independence or captivity.

If you have an audience of "independents" and your show is terrible, they simply won't watch it. An audience of "captives" creates a bigger problem. They, of necessity, must pay attention. They're expected to absorb this information and may be asked questions immediately after viewing.

What happens if your show doesn't hold their attention? The people in the audience resent it. They resent being forced to watch it. And they surely do not look upon your topic with great favor.

In both situations, you've lost your audience. And maybe it's because you didn't realize how easy they were to hold. What is this? **Why** is this?

You have a specific audience; that's what our field is all about. You don't have to dilute your message to please an audience of millions. You know who these people are. You know what they have in common and why they're watching your show.

You're taking a subject in which they're already interested (or if they're not, you've found out why and intend to tackle that) and you're glamorizing it on the screen. They really do want to watch your show. It's an adventure, a novelty, a break in the day. Don't let them down.

You have a chance to intrigue them with new information and make them feel important. When you research, you learn more and more about your audience. You realize what they know and don't know, and you discover that you know things they don't.

Think about your audience as you research. Which of these bits of information will grab their attention? How will you arrange this information so its elements unfold in an exciting way? What thoughts or feelings do you want to leave with them?

What a show can become begins with you, the writer. In its essence, a show's budget, equipment, available crew and talent matter only in how well you use them. All your work is dedicated to one goal: reaching your audience. Through your research, you must find ways to touch them.

7
Research

With any kind of writing, research is important. In our business, research is of equal, and maybe greater, importance than the writing. In a sense, they are relative: the more research you do, the better your writing can become. Why? Remember, we are writing descriptions. The more you observe, the more detailed you can make your scripts.

Research will reveal the many facets of your topic, will give it depth, and will unearth a wealth of webbings to interconnect the facts. The more research you do, the better you are able to stand back from the issue and see what's important.

If you want to become a good scriptwriter, you must become an expert researcher. At first you may have to make a conscious effort, but later research will become a habit.

Research in General

Research is a constant process. When you watch television or see a movie, a ballet, or any kind of production, be aware of the things that grab your attention, set the mood, capture an essence, carry the message strongly, or simply dazzle you.

Never miss a chance to see what other people in your field are doing. Attend some of the many video, film and multi-image conferences that are showcases for audio visual work. Check the Open Viewing at the International Television Association (ITVA) International Conference. You can also borrow programs from ITVA's Video Network and Video Exchange.

Read other people's scripts when you have a chance, and even offer to exchange scripts and finished shows with other writers in your area.

Keep a little notebook with you at all times and write down or draw pictures of things you want to remember. Keep another notebook at home by the television. Many programs and commercials are filled with ideas and production tricks you can adapt.

For example, one commercial had employees' faces, changing in rapid succession, inside the shape of the company's logo. A variation of that with a similar-shaped logo can make a nice ending for one of your shows.

Another commercial showed an artist's hand on a drawing board, sketching an outline of his company's network, accompanied by a voice over narrator. If you keep that idea and make it short and simple, you have an interesting new version of the classic "chalk talk", or a way to explain the inner workings of a machine.

Occasionally, clear out these notebooks and put all your notes into a central Idea File, or copy them into a big notebook. Many bookstores sell blank 8½ x 11 books, which are ideal for this. Such notes can inspire you when you're plumb out of ideas, and guarantee that you won't forget interesting things.

Research in Specific

That's scriptwriting research in general. Research in specific for your script is a much different matter. Your research will be immediate, condensed, detailed, time-consuming, sometimes uncomfortable and always thought-provoking.

It is very important for your information to be thorough and accurate, so you must give yourself as much research time as you can. If you keep track of the time you spend on each show, you'll find that certain patterns emerge and you will be able to estimate better how much time to allot for different kinds of programs.

The accuracy of the information you gather is critical to the show's success — and yours. There's only one thing worse than having to stop a production mid-stream because someone thinks there's a mistake in the script, and that's finding a mistake in the finished show. Revisions are expensive and also very embarrassing. Research well.

So far, this doesn't seem to be very exciting. Well, research **is** exciting. Yes, it's hard work with a great deal of responsibility, but it's also a fascinating experience.

You will be learning about your topic from experts, and with specialized topics, often the international experts. You'll soon find yourself amazed at how much you know and understand about the way things work in the world around you.

Because these experts and the facilities of the subject itself may be located in different places, you will have the opportunity to travel.

And because you're asking people about what they know best, they enjoy talking to you and you make many friends.

The Goals

Research has two main goals: to make you an expert on the subject, and to bring out the "Oh, Wow!"

"Oh, Wow?" What's that? It's that something that grabs your audience's attention and makes them sit up in their seats and say "Oh, Wow!" It is the feeling that is the essence of any exciting visual presentation. It's that transcendence, like Baryshnikov's body suddenly leaping above and across the stage or a giant, perfect-to-every-detail Campbell's soup can. It's that something that captures the viewers and impels them to pay attention.

So, when you research, you should not only be gathering information, you should be on the lookout for interesting, imaginative and audience-holding ways of presenting what you've found.

The Process

How should you research? From the beginning, you should be curious, organized and enthusiastic.

Gather Printed Information on the Subject. For example, with Employee Communications or Financial Report programs, you can review employee newspapers, magazines and annual reports. This will help you understand the information that employees receive now and will help you know more about the organization.

For shows on Employee Information, Orientation, Benefits and the like, you might look up material that tells the history of the company, and the brochures that explain specific policies. You can also check the Periodical Room in the local library to see the national and international aspect of your issue. That will help you gauge what preconceived notions the audience may already have.

If you're writing about a type of theoretical training, whether it's a concept like atomic absorption or motivation, your technical advisor will undoubtedly have a bookshelf full of material on the topic and he or she can point out the most valuable chapters or pages.

When you want printed information, just ask. The client and various technical experts usually know where abundant materials are available.

Look at Related Audio Visual Presentations. The company may have produced shows on the same topic (maybe a black/white version that's to be updated in color) or on another, similar topic. Check the organization's media files or library.

Check the ITVA Video Network or Video Exchange or similar source for shows that other companies have done on the same subject. This can help make you more familiar with your topic, and can give you an idea of how to (or how not to!) present your information.

Learn to Do What You're Trying to Show. Whether you're explaining a tool, selling a system or teaching a machine's operation, hands-on experience will give you the understanding you need to write a good script.

The classic procedure for this is: a) Watch it being done, b) Do it yourself, c) Watch it being taught and d) Teach it yourself.

One scriptwriter worked for a company for many years, learning about everything the company did from its various experts and managers. The company President once remarked, "If we ever decide to do a videotape on our Central Control Board meetings, you'll be able to run the company!"

Interview People. You must interview many people, either in person or by phone. This is extremely important. Only by talking to people will you find clues to the ways of approaching your audience. Only by talking to people will you find out what the people in the audience actually know, don't know and think about your subject. You **must** know about their attitudes and prejudices, and how your topic fits into their lives. So, these interviews are critical to your research.

For example, you might call a supervisor to ask him how he feels about Equal Employment Opportunity. He may say, "All the supervisors here think those laws are a bunch of garbage!" So, in the first few minutes of your program, you might have a "supervisor" say to a recognizable vice president, "Those laws are a bunch of garbage!" Do you think those supervisors in your audience will sit up in their seats to hear the response?

Whom should you interview? Anyone and everyone you think might have valuable information for you. They would be people like the TECHNICAL ADVISORS, who will tell you everything you wanted to know about the subject, and more.

By talking with MEMBERS OF THE PROS-
PECTIVE AUDIENCE, you'll find out what they
actually know and how they feel about the topic.
After meeting and talking with THE KINDS OF
PEOPLE THE SHOW IS ABOUT, you will be able
to portray them realistically.

Interview CUSTOMERS; you'll find out what
they're looking for in features, advantages and
benefits. PAST CUSTOMERS OR TRIAL USERS
will give you important feedback and may often
bring up problems of which the technical advisor
or client is unaware. These people can also be used
for "testimonials" in your script.

And, interview and audio tape EMPLOYEES WHO
WILL LIKELY BE ON CAMERA in your production. Then when you write for them, you can use
their own phrases and style of speaking. Since they
are not professional actors and actresses, if they
are not playing themselves, it will help if you
write roles for them which are similar to their
personalities.

How should you interview? Always prepare
questions beforehand; some people will even ask
that questions be submitted to them first.

Instead of just bringing pencil and paper, you may
want to bring a tape recorder, but always ask the
person's permission before you begin taping. Not
only will the tape recorder allow you to look at the
person instead of your notepad, it will provide you
with valuable dialogue that you can later incorporate into your script.

If you interview someone over the phone, there is a special suction device that can be put on the receiver that allows you to tape the conversation. An engineer could help you set that up.

Some writers insist that they never create any dialogue, that they pick it all up from the people they interview. That's not as preposterous as it sounds. Art Linkletter always said, "Kids say the darndest things." Well, all people say the darndest things, things you never could, or would, dream up yourself. Those wonderful comments give life, charm and reality to your script. Don't pass them up.

When you interview people in person, pay attention to visual details. Notice what people wear, how they sit, what special mannerisms they have, and what happens with their hands and eyes.

It's also interesting to find out about people's lives outside work. If a warehouse packer is the coach of a Little League team or plays the trumpet in a band on weekends, you just may want to show him in that context in your script.

Try and Visit All Locations. You will need to know where the places and people related to your topic are, and what they look like. Then you can decide where the actions will take place in your script, and you'll be able to give detailed descriptions.

Visiting locations tells you things you might never discover over the phone. For instance, say you're writing a show for and about insurance underwriters and their assistants. By visiting a local Service Office, you will see how old these people are, how they dress, if there are more men than women, how their work areas are set up, who has offices, who has cubicles, where they sit by rank in relationship to one another, what they keep on their desks and how they interact with each other.

By absorbing all this, you will be able to write those details in your script and will save the production crew headaches in casting and finding props. This will also guarantee that your scenes will be realistic. If your details are true-to-life, the audience will immediately associate with the scene. But if things are out of order or character, the audience will reject the scene as being unrealistic and will be distracted by the inconsistencies.

Sometimes no one else from the production crew will have a chance to check out the location before the shooting, so you can help them know what to expect. You can act as a scout, noting interesting shooting angles, or things that might cause problems, like insufficient lighting or cramped compartments.

If you can't visit a location, you still must know what it looks like. Try and get someone to take photographs and send them to you. At the very least, get someone to describe the place in detail over the phone.

Never leave questions unanswered as you do your research, they'll surely come up later.

In the end, you will have gathered far more information that you will ever end up using in your script, maybe ten times more. That information isn't wasted. Having that information is precisely what helps you put the subject and its many facets into the proper perspective.

The Mechanics

The mechanics of researching are, of course, a personal matter. Some people use note cards and put one thought or fact on each card. Others simply take notes on 8½ x 11 paper. Some people take shorthand or notehand. Some take tape recorders. Other people start a separate notebook for each project.

The styles of researching, as you can imagine, are endless. Try different methods, invent your own, and use what works best for you.

The important things to remember are to keep all your information on one project in one place, and to keep everything accurately labelled. Know where everything came from and who said what, when.

Now at last, you feel that your research is complete. You have become an expert on your topic and you know what will make your audience say "Oh, Wow!" You know what there is to see and hear on the matter, and you have your own thoughts and feelings about the best approaches to take.

You may not have realized it, but you already have earned a unique and creative vantage point on the subject of your script.

8
Organizing
Your Material

Your research is done. In your mind, you feel like an expert. In your office, you look like a pack rat.

In front of, above, and all around you are piled:

- A folder or notebook, full of notes from tours, interviews and phone calls.
- Papers full of other scribbled notes.
- Brochures and copies of printed material, with important segments marked and high-lighted.
- Audio cassettes, with important passages already transcribed.
- Note cards.
- Photographs.
- Miscellaneous props uncovered by research.
- Any or all of the above.

What do you do with all this? Before you can write a script, design a Treatment or do anything else with your show, you must organize all your material. Again, this is a personal matter and every writer will have his or her own system.

From this point on in the scriptwriting process, you should work in a quiet place, where you won't be interrupted or distracted.

Sorting the Material

The first thing to do is to organize your research into categories. By now, you should have some idea of the general areas your show will cover. List them, in a loose manner. They might go something like this:

1. Introduction
2. The history of the product
3. Today's line of products
4. Research and development
5. Manufacturing procedures
6. Special packaging
7. Sales network
8. Uses of product/customer benefits
9. Future of product
10. Conclusion

Once you have made this list, you need to break down your notes into these categories. This is where having your notes on index cards, one fact per card, makes life easier.

If you've done that, you simply line up your cards in categories and make little stacks. Some people use a giant corkboard and pin up all their cards in columns.

Maybe you don't have index cards. Maybe you are among those people who have a difficult time interviewing someone while shuffling a pile of cards. Or maybe you write so few words in your notes that the only way you know what you meant is to see what came before and after. Or, you had many printed pieces and brochures, which you would have had to re-copy to get on index cards. For you, index cards didn't work.

So you have pages of notes, with many different categories on each page. You can organize all this simply, too. What you can do is cut your pages apart. Actually, you should not cut your pages apart. For your protection, you should make copies and cut apart the copies.

Protection? Yes. If, for example, the technical advisor comes running back to you, pointing to a suspicious sentence in the script, saying "Where did you ever get this??!!", you will be very sorry to have the cut-apart piece of paper and not remember where, or whose interview, it came from. So, it's a good idea to make copies of your papers before you cut.

Grouping the Material

To organize all your material into categories, start with a fistful of different-colored crayons or markers. Assign a color to each of the categories on your list by putting a colored dot next to each category.

Now you can color-code all your material. Read through everything and put a pertinent colored mark next to each fact, identifying it with its proper category. Some information, you will soon realize, ought to be excluded. This is a weeding-out process, too.

Now, all of your important information has a colored dot next to it. Then take sheets of scrap paper (since you're going to cover them up, it doesn't matter what is already on them) and write a category's name at the top of each page.

Next, cut apart all the notes and tape them, in some semblance of logical order, onto the scrap papers. Staple together all the pages in the same category and voilá! You end up with nice little packets of organized material that look somewhat like patch-work quilts.

This might seem like an enormous amount of paper and tape, but the method works, especially when you're dealing with a great deal of different kinds of material.

However you do it, you must find some good system for organizing your material. Unless you know what information is to be included and how it fits together, it will be nearly impossible to write a succinct and lucid script. Your organization process may also point out "holes" in your research, which you can now proceed to fill in.

Once you have come this far, you'll find that your fingers will start itching to write.

Organizing Method

PACKAGING CONTAINERS / METHODS

PACKAGING

Packaging - specialty pkg
We were the first to have (Saje Cote)
Maybe 1st to pioneer (Saje tin)

Fisher packaging innovations, too, have meant untold savings in time, money and effort to chemists everywhere. The PolyPac™, a light-weight polyethylene bottle that dispenses reagent right from the shelf. The Gram-Pac®, a polyethylene-lined envelope containing the pre-mixed dry ingredients for a precise volume of standard solution. Vu/Slants™, sterile, prepared culture media in easy-to-handle screw-cap glass bottles, packaged in easy-viewing cartons. (They stay put, save time, and provide a full 5% more slant area while using ⅓ less incubator area.)

Packaging is an important consideration of manufacture, for the products must be able to be shipped, stored and handled with minimum breakage or damage and with minimum possible contamination change. The Company has made several packaging innovations, one of which is its Gram-Pac® system of individual, sealed packs of pre-weighed chemicals.

Automatic dispensing balances fill a GramPac.® Fisher's pioneering polyethylene-lined envelope containing the pre-mixed dry ingredients for a precise volume of standard solution. You just add water "to the mark". The storage space you save is tremendous, and the dry mixes are stable indefinitely, whereas solutions may be unstable.

PolyPac is a handy, light-weight 2- or 5-gallon polyethylene bottle that dispenses reagent right from the shelf. There's no need to transfer reagents, handling is easier and safer, chances for contamination are eliminated.

Organizing Method

Metric Gallon Cans

The 4-liter (metric gallon) Safe-Tin can is part of Fisher's continuing conversion to the metric system. Nineteen ACS grade reagents are now available in metric gallon safety cans. (See list on page 4.)

Safer because . . .
They meet OSHA* requirements for storage of flammable, hazardous reagents:

(1) Made of tin-plated steel (forget about broken bottles).

(2) Pressure-tested. Soldered seams provide complete freedom from contamination and leakage.

(3) Bright red color emphasizes the need for caution.

(4) Handle features full four-finger grip. (No slippery glass to slip and crash.)

(5) Wide mouth. (Easy pouring from brim-full containers.)

No compromise in quality . . .
Extensive shelf-life studies have been run to assure top quality performance and purity. Lot analysis data is printed directly on labels. Depend on Fisher ACS reagents for your most demanding analytical techniques.

Storeroom space savers . . .
Cases of new square metric gallons not only contain more fluid than round U.S. gallon jugs, but they occupy up to 55% less space in your storeroom.

*Occupational Safety Health Act

Color-coded buffers

SAFE-TINS

Expert packaging for safety, economy, convenience

You receive Fisher reagents in packages designed to meet every reagent requirement.

Safety is always first — unbreakable plastic bottles for compatible reagents, metal cans for flammable solvents, styrofoam liners around nitric acid bottles. All packaging meets OSHA and United States Department of Transportation regulations.

There's a size for every need — from one ounce to one ton — with emphasis on economy. The Fisher Six-Pack offers full case discounts on only six bottles, not 12. Save 25% over single bottles. Price is even better on five and 55-gallon drums. We can supply any Fisher reagent in bulk.

economy

Fisher packaging can also simplify your routine. PolyPac™, for instance, is a store-dispense container; just turn its spigot to dispense solution. Auto-Analyzer solutions — in Chemister™ Containers — fit directly into the instrument's cassette. No transferring or contamination.

Labels, coated to resist moisture, also receive special consideration. Acid labels are color-coded for quick, safe identification. And hazardous reagent labels bear safe handling and storage recommendations.

Look for even more advanced packaging in the future. Fisher packaging experts are constantly searching for safer, stronger, more economical materials and designs.

9
Looking for a Concept

Your material is organized. What do you do now? Start writing the script, logically, fact by fact? Well, you could. But your audience would probably fall asleep. For this sophisticated audience, you can't present content only and hope that they'll want to pay attention.

What you need now is a CREATIVE CONCEPT, a basic framework to tie your facts together in a creative way to hold your audience's attention.

Some people are afraid of the notion of "creativity". They think of it as inspiration, a bolt from heaven, and they fear that they will be ruined if the bolt doesn't come along before their deadlines.

The fact is, no one could make a living from writing if he or she sat around waiting for lightning bolts. What "finding a concept" really means is a manner of working from your notes. The key to this is FINDING. If you researched well, the concept is there, in your notes. All you have to do is learn to find it.

Looking for the Facts

First, be in that quiet place. Let your mind be loose. Then do what's sometimes called "solitary brainstorming", "incubation" or "stewing". Fill your mind with the material you've uncovered, then let your subconscious take over and help you draw out significant facts.

Try to put yourself in the place of the people in your audience. Then slowly read through your notes, constantly thinking about:

    What appeals to you?
    What inspires you?
    What makes you angry?
    What might persuade you to think differently?
    What didn't you know before?

Pick out the facts that you think might be your "Oh, Wows" and write them down. They might be surprises or things of unusual interest, things that will make your audience feel differently or know more about your topic.

After all, there's really only one thing in which every person in that audience is interested: WHAT'S IN IT FOR ME? You must know what to tell them.

This means that, in essence, every show is a sales show. You are "selling" the audience on an idea:

    Your job will be easier if you learn this.
    Boy, can you get in trouble if you don't watch out for that.

Do it **this** way, and you're likely to be promoted.
Help solve this problem, and things can really change.

It's all based on the old marketing adage of "Don't tell me what it does, tell me what it will do for me." That's exactly what you're doing; you are translating the facts into features, advantages and benefits for the audience.

Selecting Some Facts

As you go through your notes, write down a list of facts and read them over. They might be something like this:

Our company played an important part in our nation's history.

The manufacturing process is aesthetically beautiful.

Hiring the wrong person can get you, and the company, in trouble.

A "decision" is different from "a snap judgement". It's an involved 5-step process.

The only reason diagnostics exist is because there is disease. Disease exists because the world is not sterile.

Our system of ordering, shipping and receiving supplies never seems to work right.

Photometric analysis affects people in their daily lives — helping newborn babies, crop yields and detectives.

Distillation is a surprisingly simple process.

A person who runs this complex instrument must be a person who demands high performance.

This machine's trouble spots are well-hidden.

The company is **international.**

People at a non-union plant enjoy having diversified assignments. They don't want to belong to a union.

The metric system is relatively similar to the system you use now.

Manufacturing workers will feel more pride in their work if they see how people use the products they make.

Everything in the universe is a chemical.

We make an enormous array of products, more than most employees realize.

Customers have the support of many people, working to back them up.

You're not alone. Nearly all new supervisors feel frightened on their first day.

The last new machine in this field lasted 20 years. This one probably will, too.

This machine is very clean to operate.

This message from the company President is especially important.

The story of this sales order is intriguing.

You will probably come up with some facts that encompass the feeling of the entire show, while others relate only to the specific categories you defined when you organized your notes. All of these facts are valuable.

Next, you must find a framework or frameworks that will work with these facts.

FACT + FRAMEWORK = CONCEPT

10
Choosing a Framework

Some people come into a project with a pre-conceived framework. You'll hear remarks like, "I think I'll use puppets on this one" or "I just saw a great stand-up comic and I want to write him into my next show."

If you take a framework and simply stuff all your information inside, the framework will overpower your facts. People will remember that they saw a puppet show or a comedian, but they won't remember your message.

Instead, the framework should intrinsically evolve from and integrate with the facts you want to present. The framework should make the facts more memorable. This is not to say that you should never use puppets or comedians, it's just that there should be a good reason for it, a reason related to your facts.

Perhaps the best way to discuss frameworks is to take a look at some of the most common types used in our field today. This is by no means an exhaustive list, but examples to give you an idea of the variety of your options.

Animation, Simple or Complex. By using artwork, photographs or video or film footage, you can show how inner mechanisms work, create time lapses, display assortments of products or enliven your title. This often can be done inexpensively, using back-lit negatives and a bit of imagination and improvisation.

Artwork, Graphics, Cartoons. You can show something that cannot be seen by the naked eye, personify an issue or prove a point. Artwork previously done on the subject (in a brochure, perhaps) can usually be adopted for the screen and can reinforce the other medium.

"Chalk Talk." Blackboard-style lectures should be avoided. Unless the person and the information are compelling, your program will be terribly boring. It is possible that this message belongs on audio tape, accompanied by a booklet if necessary.

Demonstration. This, naturally, can be any number of things. The question to ask is "WHO will do the demonstrating?" The actual person who does that job may be more realistic, but may be uneasy on camera. Consider your audience's reaction to that person, to an actor, to a local newcaster or to a celebrity. Perhaps the employee can perform the demonstration, accompanied by a professional voice over narrator.

Documentary, Available or Staged Action. A documentary is meant to be an objective "documentation" of an event. There is doubt, however, whether anything can be objective when it occurs in front of a camera. The fact that the camera is there must have some effect, it seems.

If an event will occur only one time, like the yearly stockholders' meeting, it will have to be shot as is. You will probably select portions and post-script, which means to write the bridges between the portions later.

For actions that occur constantly, like people working on an assembly line, it is better to study the process and the people, select the scenes which will tell your story, and script them. In this way, the director can ask people to repeat actions (thus, they are "staged") and you will be assured that all the scenes you need to tell your story have been shot.

Drama. This will always be staged, but will usually be based on real situations. Characters will be based on people you know or have seen, and dialogue will be based on what you have heard.

Short, controversial "dramatic sequences" are often used before a Stop Tape or Discussion Break to instigate discussion on the topic.

Entertainment Parody. The following chapter treats these in more detail, since they appear deceptively easy, yet have the greatest chance of failure. The most popular kinds of parodies have been: clowns, comedies, commercials, detective stories, game shows, magic shows, mimes, personifications, puppet shows and Westerns.

Interview. This is a good way to elicit startling information or testimonials. As with documentaries, they may be either spontaneous or prepared. As with demonstrations, the main concern is "WHO is this person and how important is what he or she has to say?"

Some annoying problems that happen with interviews are that people tend to ramble, and often look too far off-camera at the interviewer. To avoid this somewhat, plan your interview questions well and try for more eye contact with the camera.

Montage. When you have a series of visual images whose message is self-explanatory, a way of presenting that is to show them in a montage set to music. The tone and the type of images will dictate the kind of music, which in turn will dictate the rhythm and flow. Of course, montages can also have voice over narration.

On-Camera Narrator. This person can take the audience on a tour, serve as a bridge between sequences, give background materials, present demonstrations, create a specific image or tie your entire show together. When deciding to use an on-camera narrator, it's important to decide upon age, sex, "costume" and effect on the audience. Perhaps have a person or two in mind.

Newscast. If you are doing a regular TV News show for your organization, you will probably incorporate the network-style frameworks, such as: anchorperson, chroma keys, interviews, "on the scene" reports and editorials.

If you are not doing a regular TV News show and you are planning to parody a News format for another kind of show, examine your conscience. You are taking a lazy way out and you shouldn't do it. Try and find a better way to present that information.

Panel Discussion. This is much like the "chalk talk". It is essentially boring to watch and unless there is some very lively and controversial back-and-forth among significant and highly recognizable people, it probably belongs in another medium.

Slides, Photographs. Very often interesting visuals are available to you in these forms and they can be made very exciting by a good editor using camera moves, cuts, dissolves and special effects.

Special Effects. In video, they are usually dictated by the console used in the editing process. Find out what is available and how you might best use them. In film, most are expensive. Beware of using effects for effects' sake; you can end up with a flashy, but unmemorable program.

Some kinds of effects available might be: chroma key, split screen, geometric inserts, computer animation, color polarizations, discs for slowed or speeded action, and more.

Stock Footage. There are stock footage companies in both film and video which, for a small sum, can provide you with scenes of just about everything from the solar system to a Mexican hat dance.

Subjective Camera. This is sometimes called "point of view" and it means that the camera sees things from the actor's, or your, point of view. It is usually used in reaction shots or for limited sequences, and not throughout an entire show.

Symbolism, Metaphor. You can take any recognizable symbol and create new meanings. You might use toy cars and trucks to show an accident, or a river to represent the flow of ideas. The possibilities are unlimited.

"Talking Head". The "Talking Head", which is a shot of a person talking directly to the camera, is perhaps the most misused and over-used of all frameworks. Talking heads should only be used for significance — of the person, the message, or both. More important, they should only be used for very brief periods. Fifteen seconds or less is fine, 30 seconds gets to be boring and 60 seconds (or more!) is inexcusable.

Tour. A tour can be spatial, which means going from place to place, or it can be chronological, leading the viewer through time. With tours, there must be some sort of guide, whether on or off camera.

These and other frameworks, and combinations of them, will work as the basis for your program's design.

11
Entertainment
Frameworks

Entertainment frameworks deserve special attention because they can turn out the best, and the worst, of shows.

If you do a superb job of a comedy, a drama or a puppet show, it is wonderful. However, anything less than superb is deadly. A dull comedy, a poorly-acted drama or a silly puppet show is far more obnoxious than a simple, straightforward and even boring production.

Just because a show is in an entertainment style doesn't automatically make it entertaining. In fact, almost the opposite occurs. You set yourself up to be compared with Hollywood, and you have a lot farther to fall.

There have been a number of notable ITVA award-winning shows that have successfully used entertainment styles. Among them are Hewlett-Packard's jugglers in "Solving Group Problems", Olin's mime in "Office Safety", Pacific Northwest

64

Bell's" clown in "In Case There's a Fire", Fisher Scientific's commercial parodies and Broadway Department Store's "Customer Service with the Marx Brothers." In each of these instances the treatment emerged from, and was intrinsic to, the message.

To be successful, you must go beyond having an intrinsic message. If you are imitating entertainment, you must first figure out for yourself what makes entertainment entertaining.

For instance, perhaps you want to write a comedy. You've chosen to do a version of "Laugh-In", Steve Martin, Laurel and Hardy, "All in the Family" or "Saturday Night Live". Before you go one step farther, you must make certain that there will be someone willing, able and affordable to play those roles.

If you will have the performers, your next step is to analyze what it is that makes what you want to imitate funny. Is it the "costume"? The mannerisms? The pacing? Are there three lines, then a punch line? Are you tricked into thinking one thing will happen, then just the opposite occurs?

If you want to use puppets, you better study them. Clowns? Analyze them, too. A magician? What makes the illusions fascinating? The same goes for Game Shows, commercials, film stars and the like.

If you want to write a drama, you must first understand the classic underpinnings of drama: conflict, dilemma, climax and resolution. You must be a story-teller and know how to create and develop characters. This is especially difficult, since the characters will only be known for 10 or 15 minutes.

You must also know how to write realistic dialogue, and how to pace the action and create meaning from the way people act, instead of what they say.

None of this is easy, although it seems like such fun. Understand the difficulties before you begin. Most writers have, at one time or another, written scripts that later cause them to cringe. Into which category do you think most of them fall?

In entertainment frameworks, more than ever, you as a writer need a "mentor", someone you like and respect who will be honest with you. Try your script out on this person. Does he or she laugh, or get caught up in your story so it's impossible to set it aside? Get some honest reactions. If people you respect have qualms about this parody you've written, please hesitate to use it.

Sophisticated. Sophisticated. Sophisticated. Repeat ten times before venturing on any Hollywood-style productions.

12
Settling on a Concept

Frameworks are the structures for your facts and you can use them in all sorts of combinations. You can take one framework and weave your entire show through it, as with a drama. Or, you can have a number of segments, each with its own framework, but tied together by an overall framework. Thus, you might have a narrator tying together segments that include slides, a demonstration, a montage and interviews.

The framework(s) you choose should be the best and most memorable way you can think of to present your facts.

To give you some idea of how FACT + FRAMEWORK combine to create your CONCEPT, here are some ideas which were developed from the facts given before.

FACT	FRAMEWORK	CONCEPT
Our company has played an important part in our nation's history.	Montage, Photographs	A montage of camera moves and quick cuts on old sepiatone photographs from the company's library and old catalogs. (segment)
The manufacturing process is aesthetically beautiful.	Montage	A montage of video footage, showing the process with classical music in the background. (segment)
Hiring the wrong person can get you and the company in trouble.	Drama	A drama illustratting supervisors hiring, firing and promoting the wrong people. (entire show)
A "decision" is different from a "snap judgement". It's an involved, 5-step process.	Drama	A drama showing someone forced to go through the decision-making process. (entire show)

FACT	FRAMEWORK	CONCEPT
The only reason diagnostics exist is because there is disease.	Parody	A parody of a party scene in a "sterile" world. (introduction)
Our system of ordering, shipping and receiving supplies never seems to work right.	Game Show	The process of supply is like a Game of Chance. (introduction)
Photometric analysis affects people in their daily lives.	Documentary	Brief, documentary-style scenarios to depict three occurrences. (introduction)
Distillation is a very simple process.	Animation, Artwork	Simple animation of artwork illustrates the process. (segment)
A person who runs this complex instrument must demand high performance.	Narrator	A series of scenes with representative narrator driving a high-performance car. (introduction)

FACT	FRAMEWORK	CONCEPT
This machine's trouble spots are well-hidden.	Artwork	Artwork, with highlights of trouble spots. (segment)
The company is **international.**	Special Effect	A six-way split screen of people answering the phone in different languages. (segment)
People at a non-union plant enjoy having diversified assignments.	Documentary	A documentary of people at work with their voice-overs telling how they feel about that work. (entire show)
The metric system is similar to the one you use now.	Parody	A Magic Show, using illusions to demonstrate the similarities. (entire show)
Manufacturing workers should see how people use the things they make.	Special Effect	A split screen, showing people making products and people using them. (segment)

FACT	FRAMEWORK	CONCEPT
Everything in the universe is a chemical.	Symbolism	A globe gets smaller until it becomes a dot (crystal) which joins a shower of crystals coming from a chemical vial. (introduction)
We make an enormous array of products.	Simple Animation	Pop on, quickly, one by one, many products until they fill the screen. (segment)
Customers have the support of many people.	Narrator, Symbolism	See a narrator at different times, each time with more and more people behind him. (series of segments)
All new supervisors feel frightened that first day.	Subjective Camera	A subjective camera fish-eye lens makes everything on that first day look frightening. (introduction)
The new machine will probably last 20 years.	Parody	A Space Lab saga, showing the machine in use in the year 2000. (entire show)

FACT	FRAMEWORK	CONCEPT
Accidents cause enormous day-to-day headaches for supervisors.	Documentary	Recreate scenes of accidents and follow through effects on supervisors. (series of segments)
This machine is very clean to operate.	Narrator, Demonstration	The narrator wears a white suite while demonstrating machine. (segment)
This message from the president is very important.	Talking Head	Talking head of president delivering brief message. (segment)
The story of this sales order is intriguing.	Documentary	A documentary follows through the story of the order. (entire show)

Finding a concept is perhaps the most exhilarating and intense part of the scriptwriting process. The concepts you come up with are limited only by your imagination, overshadowed by your budget and resources.

What about Budget?

Writing within budget is, at its simplest, a complex issue. Undoubtedly, you will be given a budget. The question is, what does that budget mean?

In some organizations, the amount given as your budget will only have to cover out-of-pocket expenses. That means that all of the organization's resources, which may include an audio visual staff, artists, location and studio equipment, and editing facilities are "free". Other organizations use a charge-back system, and your budget may have to include even staff salaries and overhead.

Every organization has different resources and handles the situation differently. When you are given a budget, the critical issue is: WHAT MUST THESE DOLLARS PAY FOR? You must find out if your budget will have to include:

- Staff salaries
- Overhead
- Studio equipment
- Location equipment
- Editing facilities
- Rental equipment, if the department's isn't sufficient for the job
- Artwork
- Location shooting expenses, including transportation, meals and lodging
- Actors, actresses
- Costumes and props
- Tape or film stock (and film lab fees)

- Music and sound effects (original or library)
- Set design and construction
- Photography
- Anything else your script might require

You must find out which of these things your budget dollars will have to cover, then balance your resources as you write your script. For instance, you might have four actors with all scenes occurring in a warehouse, as opposed to one actor in twelve locations. Maybe you'll use all employees for talent, then incorporate a lot of artwork and library music.

You will always be playing this game of juggling resources. The challenge is to use them, and your talents, to ingeniously create the most effective show possible.

Selecting Your Concept

You have taken your list of facts and developed each within producible frameworks. Now you have a list of concepts. Go through all these ideas, thinking: Which best communicates your message? Which will best hold the audience's attention. Which are realistically within your budget and production capabilities?

At least a few of your concepts should be viable. Pick the one that you think works best. Do you like it? If you don't like it now, you'll hate it later. And don't expect it to be saved in production.

If you don't feel comfortable or excited about any of your concepts, repeat the brainstorming process until you find one you do like and want to develop. Then talk to the production people to make sure it's workable.

Next, you ought to approach your client with your idea and your reason for choosing it. Some people wonder whether or not it's better to present a few concepts. If you do, you'll find that it weakens your presentation, takes time away from thinking through your best idea, and makes you look like you can't make up your mind. Present one idea, then have others ready as alternatives should the client not like the one you chose.

Does your client like the idea? If not, chances are he or she will hate it later, too. If the client doesn't like the idea and you try to insist upon it, you're asking for trouble, because more than likely the client will continue to have objections the entire way through the scripting and approval process. Sometimes the client may like an idea, but may know reasons why it won't work. It's better to find that out now.

If everyone gives you the go-ahead, you can breathe your first sigh of relief. If you're honestly happy with your concept now, it's pretty certain that you'll be happy with your script.

13
The Working Outline: The Show's Design

Surely **now** it's time to begin writing the script, isn't it? Well, not quite. Before you can write your show you must first design it, as a visual and auditory experience. You must look at the big picture of what you have to show and say, and arrange the presentation of that information with a rhythm and flow that will hold the audience's attention.

You will need a GRABBER at the beginning, naturally, to grab the audience's attention. For example, in an employee orientation program for a truck company, you might begin with an exciting, fast-paced 45-second history.

Then you need some kind of CONTINUITY, which will lead to a conclusion. This continuity might be a story. In a drama it would mean conflict, crisis and resolution. It may be a passing through time, or through space, like a tour. Continuity may be posed as problem and solution, or cause and effect. In any case, it must develop throughout your show, and reach a conclusion. For the program for truck company employees, you could weave the concept of "truck builders" through all your information.

Your show must end with a STINGER, something that is quick, sharp and memorable, and will make your show's message stick in people's minds. In the truck program, you might create a striking visual to reinforce your theme.

Avoid "Glom" Shows

Once you've thought through the continuity you want to develop, there is yet another step. Too many shows today look like "Glom" shows. The entire show, from beginning to end, is glommed together so that it all looks the same, sounds the same and feels the same.

"Glom" shows lose the audience because there is nothing new to spark their interest. If your show is monotonously spewing forth information, it doesn't take long to turn off the audience.

So, what you must do is design the presentation of this information to wake up or re-grab the audience every few minutes. How do you do this? You do it by giving your show internal variations.

You go from fast to slow, from live action to graphics, from somber to excited, from quiet to loud, from "heavy" information to breathing room, and so forth. You change the pace to surprise the audience. What you're really saying is "Pay attention, here's something new." "That's over, here's something else new."

It's been said that the only reason people read books all the way to end is because they want to find out what happens next. If people are sure that nothing new is going to happen or if they've guessed what will happen, they lose interest. The same thing goes for our audiences. If they think that what will happen next will be just a continuation of what's happening now, they lose interest.

What that means for you is that even if what you're writing about is a simple 1-2-3-4 process, you don't want to present it as simply 1-2-3-4. You must alter that straightforward simplicity to hold your audience's attention.

The way to do that is to design your show with clearly distinguishable segments, or "acts", if you will, as in a play. People should know, by the music fading out, the words you use or the feeling of the action that this segment is definitely ended. Yet their curiosity should be aroused over what will come next.

Arranging the Information

What are these segments or acts? Where do they come from? Well, when you organized your material, you divided it into different categories. For instance, the segments in the show for the truck company might be:

1. History of the Company
2. Our Trucks Today
3. A Custom Truck Order
4. Parts Manufacturing

5. Truck Manufacturing
6. Dealer/Sales/Parts Network
7. Corporate Support
8. Conclusion

What you will do now is use these categories to write a Working Outline. This is an exercise designed to help you ferret out the information to be imparted, and to design the presentation of that information in conjunction with visuals, and your intended audience effect.

Take a sheet of paper, divide it into three columns and work through each of your categories in terms of what you're trying to get across in each. For each of your categories, think about three things: the INFORMATION to be imparted, what EFFECT you want to have on the audience, and what you might SHOW to get across the information, to get the audience to think, feel or know the things you want. At the end of this chapter, there is a Working Outline for the script on the truck company's program.

Writing such a Working Outline will help you to see the big picture of what you are designing and will give you ideas for internal variations. You can avoid putting similar segments together. If you're using a narrator, you can see if you have created a natural pattern of appearance.

Things you want to repeat for effect can be paced evenly. You can see whether you've woven your concept effectively throughout the show. And you can examine where music and special sounds might be incorporated.

This Working Outline also forces you to think about whether the visuals you plan to show are the best ways of illustrating your information to achieve the desired effects.

Solving Problems

Perhaps now is the time to address two frequent problems of in-house productions, because these problems should begin to be solved as you develop your Working Outline. The problems are: WORDI—NESS and EXCESSIVE LENGTH.

Your Working Outline is forcing you to tell your story through your visuals, so it should help you to avoid having ineffective images coupled with a barrage of narration. This will be discussed further in the "Audio" segment of Chapter 15.

Length is another critical area. It's been said that there ought to be a "10 Minute Rule" for in-house productions, that no program should be longer than ten minutes. About that time, audiences begin to squirm in their seats. If your show lasts much longer than that, it must be very powerful or snappy to hold their attention.

Ten minutes is a long time. It's equivalent to **twenty** television commercials and one-third of the evening news. Handled well, almost anything can, and often should, fit into ten minutes.

As you develop your Working Outline, be concerned with the number and length of your segments. If you realize that you have 23 segments, you can imagine that such a program would end up longer than ten minutes. Then, you must think about alternatives, like eliminating segments or suggesting that the material be divided into two programs.

You also can estimate the timing of each segment as you go along. This will make you more conscious of how long each segment really needs to be, and will let you know that you're actually preparing to write a 45-minute program when you were asked to do an eight-minute one. By analyzing your outline in this way, you can avoid creating an overly-long show.

Once you have thought through your Working Outline, you may or may not want to review it with your producer or your client. For the most part, it is simply an exercise to help you develop a better show and to prepare you for writing the Treatment.

WORKING OUTLINE
"The Truck Builders"

Employee Orientation Program

"THE TRUCK BUILDERS"

PURPOSE OF PROGRAM:

To inform the viewer of the corporation's scope through a presentation of its history, products, organization, manufacturing and philosophy.

To create a feeling that this is a good company to work for, and a company on the move.

To instill a sense of pride.

AUDIENCE:

Primary: New or prospective employees (including campus recruitment).

Secondary: Current employees, dealers, customers, financial groups, local and civic organizations.

VISUALS	INFORMATION	AUDIENCE EFFECT
1. COMPANY'S HISTORY		
Exciting, fast-moving montage of old photos, tracing the company's history and its trucks.	1929. Leland James started Consolidated Truck Lines.	Attention-grabbing opening.
	1939. Began building his own trucks: Freightways. Revolutionary design.	Knowledge of company's past.
Lively, 1930's-style music.		Feeling of pride in its accomplishments.
	Over the years, other revolutionary designs followed.	
2. THE COMPANY TODAY		
See truck; dynamic transition from its logo to company headquarters.	General facts about the company.	Amazement at size and importance of the company.
		First impression of truck.
Scenes of people working.	The company's people: In plants In offices	Sense of appreciation for people who work here.

"The Truck Builders"

VISUALS	INFORMATION	AUDIENCE EFFECT
More scenes of people working.	In Parts Distribu- tion Centers Dealers	A good feeling about the company and its people.
End sequence with close-up of logo.	ALL TRUCK BUILDERS	

3. THE TRUCKS

Classical-style music. Two trucks lit to look elegant.	Point out COE and Conventional models.	Information about the two kinds of trucks.
Slowly dissolving montage of trucks with cutaways il-lustrating high-tech engineering and testing.	Establish these trucks as the ultimate in looks and workmanship.	Feelings of excitement and pride for these magnificent trucks.

4. AN ORDER BEGINS

Follow a customer into a dealership.	The story of how every truck is customized:	Understanding of the truck's importance to customer.
Lip sync inter-spersed with narra-tion as dealer and customer spec the order in detail.	A customer meets with a dealer and they discuss specs.	Amazement at how much truck is customized.

5. THE SPECS TAKE SHAPE

The order is given a serial number (#25000).	A condensed version of following the order:	Appreciation of the work involved in customization.
Follow that number through a sequence of fast-paced cuts showing the pro-ceedings.	-From dealer to Sales Office -Into computer -Spec writers -Frame charters -Custom engineers -Computer connected to Parts Manufacturing Plant	Understanding of the employees' roles.

"The Truck Builders"

VISUALS	INFORMATION	AUDIENCE EFFECT
6. PARTS MANUFACTURING		
Music segues into a lively, fast-paced sound.	A truck is only as good as the quality of its parts.	Appreciation of the people as master craftsmen.
Series of scenes designed to show high skill in craftsmanship, and sophisticated engineering.	That quality comes from the people who make them.	Also, feelings of manufacturing sophistication.
End with part being packed into box.		
7. TRUCK MANUFACTURING		
Follow the part in the box to specs on printout for #25000.	From the parts, the truck is built.	Understanding of how a custom truck is built.
Then follow truck assembly, highlighting workers' skills. Continually show the #25000 as the cab and chassis are assembled.	Two assembly lines-separate for cab and chassis. People work in total synchronization. Parts must fit to fraction of an inch.	Amazement at its complexity.
8. THE FINISHED TRUCK		
Sense of drama and excitement as owner admires new truck, gets in and drives off. Lip sync, natural sounds.	The completion of the truck order: The dealer presents the truck to the customer. Show off exterior and interior.	Sense of pride as new owner admires and claims his truck.
9. DEALER/SALES/PARTS NETWORK		
4-way split screen of continually-changing stills.	Hundreds of independent dealers from coast to coast.	A sense of the multitude of dealers.

"The Truck Builders"

VISUALS	INFORMATION	AUDIENCE EFFECT
Stills give a sense of variety and size and geographic location.	They sell and service the trucks.	
Match dissolve from final still to live action at dealership.	Parts Express: Computers, Inventory Warehouses, Dealers, Mechanics	Importance of parts service. Admiration of excellent system.
Quick-cutting scenes show the Network.		

10. ADDITIONAL CORPORATE SUPPORT

Scenes of different people in their departments working on trucks.	-Accounting -Engineering -Marketing -Technical Publications -Photography -Training	Including people in "desk jobs" at corporate headquarters as Truck Builders.

11. TRUCKS IN USE TODAY

Country-Western style music. Narration lead-in, then music UP over a variety of scenes of trucks travelling down the highways.	Variety of uses: Produce, steel, chemicals, refrigeration cars and so forth.	Appreciation and amazement of all the different trucks. For employees, a sense of pride in having built them.

12. CONCLUSION

Screens-full of close-ups of people; a few phrases in summary.	An appreciation of the employees.	A good feeling about the company and its people.
Lead into glimmery logo and Title.	A feeling of success and pride, confidence in the future.	

14
The Treatment

Once you've gone through the exercise of the Working Outline and you're happy with your work, you can write your script Treatment. If you have not come from a film background, you may not even know what this is. A Treatment is a narrative outline which describes in sentence form what will be seen, and the essence of what will be heard, in your show.

Usually the Treatment is the first formal, written version of what you plan to do with this program, and it's definitely subject to client approval.

Some concepts never go beyond a Treatment. Writing this Treatment, however, is the only way you can really put your script ideas to the test.

Actually, this Treatment is just a condensed version of your script. It can be written any number of ways, and you will probably find yourself doing each one a little differently. Sometimes it may be more like an ordinary outline, expanding on the points to be covered. Other times, the Treatment may read like a short story. It can be as brief as one or two pages, or it may be fifteen or twenty pages and exceed the length of the script which follows.

Writing the Treatment

When you write the Treatment, begin with a cover page citing the name of the show and the date of this Treatment. Next, include a Requirements Page which reiterates some of the show's basic elements: the purpose, audience, people involved in the production, content, and possibly the schedule.

You may want to add a special Introduction or Rationale to explain the approach you have taken. For example, perhaps you have designed a show on emergency planning so that it is told from the viewpoint of a guard. Here, you can justify your reasons for doing so, i.e., the guard is the center of all activity, a majority of the audience will be guards and will associate with this character, and so forth.

After that, you begin the body of the Treatment. Just as you would have categories in an outline, you should have the same kind of segments or "play acts".

Each of these segments should include such basic information as:

The Nature of the Sets or Scenes. Where is this taking place? Is it at the manufacturing plant? Is it in the studio? What is it we are seeing? What does it look like? What impression will it leave?

The Talent. Where do people play a part in this script? Who are they? What do they look like? Sound like? What are they wearing?

Each Segment's Development. How does the segment begin? What action takes place during the scene? What happens next? How do you know the scene is over? What is the transition to the next segment?

The Train of Thought or Key Lines of Copy. What is the message to be imparted? What is the gist of what the people will be saying? If you have already thought of phrases for the narration or important bits of dialogue, you can include them.

Major Technical Devices. Will there be animation? Special effects? Old silent footage? What else?

Write each of your segments with as much detail as you can. This will bring out the weaknesses in your design and will make your script easier to write. If you can't get your ideas to work now, they won't work later.

Essentially, the Treatment is written for the client, so it should be geared to what that person will understand. More than anything, it should give as thorough a picture as possible of what the proposed show will look and feel like.

Presentation

After you've written your Treatment, make sure that everything is typed neatly and accurately, and perhaps put in a folder. You've done a lot of careful, excellent work so far. Why not let it look that way.

A copy of this Treatment should go to the producer and director, but you should, if possible, present the client's Treatment in person. This is because the Treatment must be thoroughly approved by the client before you can use it as the basis for your script. You must talk this Treatment over with the client, see what he or she likes and doesn't like, and decide what changes to make before you put your time and energy into writing the script.

Plan a meeting with the client, perhaps for an hour or two. Bring the Treatment and all your notes. Read the entire piece aloud, even the introductory pages. Talk it through completely. Make changes, suggestions and compromises. Agree upon what is to be done and save yourself, and your client, from surprises later.

SCRIPT TREATMENT
"Decision-Making"

Donna Matrazzo
Scripts and Concepts

The Westbury #1101
271 South 15th Street
Philadelphia, PA 19102
(215) 545-2896

"DECISION-MAKING"

SCRIPT TREATMENT

(Date)

"Decision-Making"

VIDEOTAPE REQUIREMENTS

PURPOSE: To teach viewers the basic steps involved
         in the decision-making process:
         Getting the facts
         Verifying them
         Identifying the real problem
         Finding possible solutions
         Deciding upon a solution

         To instigate discussion on the facets
         of decision-making.

AUDIENCE: All company supervisors (office and plant)

REQUESTED BY: (Client's name, phone number and location)

TECHNICAL ADVISORS: (Advisors' names, numbers and
                    locations)

PRODUCER:

DIRECTOR:

WRITER:

STATUS:

Script Treatment:

Rough Script:

Production Planning Meeting:

Final Script:

Shooting Dates:

Final Edit:

Copies for Distribution:

"Decision-Making"

SCRIPT TREATMENT

PART I

Open on a scene in a branch warehouse. A fork lift
truck is weaving down the aisles. Dissolve a few
such scenes to indicate time lapse. Then the fork
lift weaves and crashes into the edge of shelving.
Boxes fall on the floor, bottles inside break and
the contents spill. Maybe all of this is silent,
except for the sound of the crash.

The foreman enters the scene, at the far end of the
aisle. He asks one of the warehousemen what happened.
The man answers that the new driver had been looking
and acting drunk all morning, and then he ran into
the shelves.

The foreman quickly walks down the aisle to the scene;
the driver looks bleary-eyed and can hardly stand.
The foreman tells the man he's drunk and he's fired
and asks the warehouseman to drive him home.

The foreman walks into the operations manager's
office and tells him he fired the new driver, and why.

STOP TAPE: DISCUSSION BREAK

> You are the foreman.
> What should you do now?

> (Discussion should bring out the point
> that the first process in decision-making
> is getting the facts.)

PART II

Open on the foreman, still in the operation manager's
office.

The operations manager re-states the information the
foreman has given him and begins to ask questions:
You said he was drunk -- Did you see him drink? Did
anyone see him drink? Did you talk to his co-workers?

"Decision-Making"

Is this the first time you've had any problem with
him? He's fairly new; have you looked at his records
from other jobs?, and so forth. The manager tries
to get as much information as possible from the
foreman.

Proceed with a series of cuts as the foreman gets
answers from various places -- the records, other
supervisors, co-workers, etc. These comments will
often contradict each other, like: "I've seen him
look drunk lots of times." and "Nope. Said he
never touches a drop." There are no clues from
past employment references. The foreman keeps
talking to people and checking his files and records.

The sequence ends with a grim-faced foreman walking
into the operations manager's office with a folder
of papers and a book. He pulls out one sheet from
the folder -- the driver's medical record. Highlight
"diabetes". He then opens a medical encyclopedia
to the page on diabetes. Highlight: "... an insulin
shock reaction takes on the appearance of intoxication
..." The foreman and operations manager look at
each other.

STOP TAPE: DISCUSSION BREAK

>   You are the foreman.
>   What should you do now?
>
>   (Discussion should bring out the points
>   that the decision-maker must get the
>   information, but assume that at least
>   some of the information will be incorrect.
>   Then, try to verify the facts so that
>   the real problem can be identified.)

PART III

Open on the foreman, again in the operations manager's
office. The operations manager asks more questions
to draw out the foreman's thoughts on the matter and
his ideas for possible solutions. Should the man remain
fired? Should he be brought back? Should he keep the
fork lift job? They discuss limitations on each
thought.

"Decision-Making"

They agree that the foreman should talk to the fork
lift driver face-to-face. They set a specific time
to meet again.

The foreman and fired driver are in a cafeteria. The
driver explains that his diabetes had been under
control for years. He contritely admits that he was
taking a chance, but thought it was slight. He
realizes that he was irresponsible; he could've hurt
himself and other people. They discuss problems
faced now on both sides.

STOP TAPE: DISCUSSION BREAK

> You are the foreman.
> The decision is ultimately in
> your hands. What should you
> do now?
>
> (Discussion should bring out the
> points that the decision-maker should
> recognize limitations on the solution,
> think about possible solutions and
> test or discuss them.)

PART IV

The foreman walks into the operations manager's office.
They talk, but we don't hear them. Repeat significant
previous scenes, using Voice-Overs and Supers to
re-cap the decision-making process:

> -Get all the facts
> -Verify the facts
> -Identify the real problem
> -Cite restrictions on the solution
> -Solicit possible solutions
> -Test/discuss solutions
> -Make decisions: overall and
> specific plans of action

End with the fork lift driver and the foreman walking
down a hallway.

SCRIPT TREATMENT
"The Truck Builders"

Donna Matrazzo
Scripts and Concepts

The Westbury #1101
271 South 15th Street
Philadelphia, PA 19102
(215) 545-2896

Freightliner Corporation

"THE TRUCK BUILDERS"

(Employee Orientation Program)

SCRIPT TREATMENT

(Date)

"The Truck Builders"

VIDEOTAPE REQUIREMENTS

PURPOSE: To inform the viewer of the corporation's scope through a presentation of its history, products, organization, manufacturing and philosophy.

To create a feeling that this a good company to work for, and a company on the move.

To instill a sense of pride.

AUDIENCE: PRIMARY: New or prospective employees (including campus recruitment).

SECONDARY: Current employees, dealers, customers, financial groups, local and civic organizations.

REQUESTED BY: (Client's name, number and location)

PRODUCER/DIRECTOR: (Name, number and location)

WRITER: (Name, number)

SCHEDULE:

Script Treatment: (Date)
Rough Script
Final Script:
Production Planning Meeting:
Shooting Dates:
Edit Date(s):
Final Presentation:
Distribution:

Shelf life of program: At least five years

"The Truck Builders"

SCRIPT TREATMENT

PART 1. THE HISTORY OF THE COMPANY

We begin with an exciting, fast-paced montage
of old slides and photographs that trace the company's history, set to lively, 1930's-style music
with lots of plinking piano. The voice over Narrator
has a deep voice, and the sound track is embellished
with sounds appropriate to the visuals (horns
honking, engines revving, etc.)

With sparse verbiage, the Narrator tells the
story: In 1929, Leland James established Consolidated
Truck Lines. For ten years, he searched in vain for
a truck to meet his demands. Finally he designed
his own -- the revolutionary Freightways. Its alu-
minum and cab-over-engine design made it four feet
shorter and a ton lighter than anything on the road
at the time. The name changed to Freightliner and
revolutionary changes have continued.

PART 2. FREIGHTLINER TODAY

The music segues into a quieter, but still
fast-paced sound. A new truck turns a corner off in
the distance, then heads directly toward the camera
and stops just as the logo on the grille is full-
screen. Inside the logo, we matte a continually
changing sequence of people at work -- at headquarters,
in plants, distribution centers and dealerships.

The Narration provides impressive statistics
about the company, then creates a feeling of the
importance of the people who work there.

They are all Truck Builders.

"The Truck Builders"

PART 3. THE FREIGHTLINER TRUCKS

The music segues into a classical, drum-heavy sound. With a black background, we create a visually elegant scene of two trucks (COE and Conventional), their chrome glimmering from star filters and colored spotlights.

Slow dissolves and pans show richness in every detail. Quick cutaways illustrate various elements of sophisticated engineering and testing.

The Narrator describes these as the Ultimate Trucks and talks in superlatives of their beauty, ruggedness and efficiency.

PART 4. AN ORDER BEGINS

A customer comes into a dealership and works with the dealer to order his custom truck.

Their conversation is interspersed with descriptive narration. The music is replaced by background sounds.

PART 5. TRUCK SPECS TAKE SHAPE

A series of fast-paced cuts follows the ordering process from the dealer to headquarters (and its sales office, spec writers, frame charters, engineers, computers) to the truck plant. We end with a match dissolve from a specs/schedule printout at the plant to a copy of the printout at the dealer's.

Background sounds and lively music accompany the narration, which briefly explains the process. The dealer calls the customer and tells him of his truck's completion schedule.

"The Truck Builders"

PART 6. PARTS MANUFACTURING

We go to scenes of parts manufacturing, showing sophisticated machinery, but with an overall attitude of revealing craftsmanship and people in control.

Music and natural sounds continue as the Narrator talks about how a truck's quality begins with its parts, and how every person here takes responsibility for trying to make every part perfect. The sequence ends with an item packed inside a "Parts" box.

PART 7. TRUCK MANUFACTURING

The "Parts" box is opened at the truck plant and we follow the part, and the truck as it is built. We create the feeling that this immense truck is being built rapidly before our very eyes.

We also focus on the skills and exactitude of the people on the lines.

The Narrator explains how the parts become the machine: with the two assembly lines, the skilled and versatile people, and the complex equipment.

PART 8. THE FINISHED PRODUCT

The magnificent new truck is parked outside the dealership. The dealer presents it to the customer, who walks around admiring it, then jumps in and takes it for a drive.

We create a sense of excitement and pride. There is no narrative; the sound track is comprised of lively music, background sounds and lip sync conversation.

"The Truck Builders"

PART 9. <u>DEALER/SALES/PARTS NETWORK</u>

We go to a four-way split screen of continually changing (still) scenes of dealerships and dealers, giving a sense of their diversity. The music segues into a different fast-paced sound and the Narrator talks about the hundreds of dealers.

Then, one of the final quadrants becomes full screen and live action; other scenes follow to illustrate the Parts Express network.

The Narrator describes the importance of parts and service, and the company's system, called "the best in the business".

PART 10. <u>ADDITIONAL CORPORATE SUPPORT</u>

Following the "Truck Builders" theme, we show scenes of people in headquarters, "building" trucks through their jobs -- in Accounting, Technical Publications, Training and so forth.

The Narrator reinforces their "truck-building" functions.

PART 11. <u>TRUCKS IN USE TODAY</u>

A diverse array of trucks drive along highways; shots are taken from different angles as the trucks whoosh past the camera. Music segues into a country-western style with lots of banjo and fiddle.

The Narrator introduces the sequence by saying how people here are proud of the trucks they build. They see them everywhere.

Music comes up and continues over the rest of the truck scenes.

"The Truck Builders"

PART 12. CONCLUSION

The screen is filled with a grid of close-up
photos of 30 to 40 people. We wipe diagonally,
twice, revealing more people.

The Narrator talks about Freightliner people:
At first courageous, building such a revolutionary
truck; then proud, as that truck was copied; now
wise, as theirs is the truck of the future.

The program ends with a glimmery chrome logo
supered over the final grid of photos. The photos
fade and the title, "The Truck Builders" appears.
The mellow music crescendoes, then fades.

15
The Video and the Audio

It has been said that if a program is well-produced, you can turn off the sound and still understand the story. Consider, then, your script. It might follow that one should be able to read just the "visuals" of your script, and still get your message.

That is perhaps a bit too simple to be true, but the notion is correct. Your visuals should carry the message. Because of that, you must write your script in a way that might seem amazing: for every scene, you should write the spoken words **last**. Use your visuals, non-verbal messages, sound effects and music to say as much as possible. Then, let the spoken words complement them.

What happens when you write the spoken words first? You begin by dividing your page into two columns. You call the right side AUDIO and you fill it up with sentences that completely say what you want to say. Then you go to the left side called VIDEO and, in essence, "fill in the video blanks".

What do you have? A VIDEO SLIDE SHOW! There might be a long shot of a building, a close-up of a notebook, a person in an office talking on the phone, and maybe four words when you couldn't think of anything else to show. It's a dreadful, confusing amalgamation of pictures, with no visual continuity and no feeling. That wouldn't happen if you'd thought of the visuals first.

The Visuals

Not every scene needs spoken words at all. Does it seem absurd that you might have a page or two of a script with no spoken words? Does it seem crazy to think of scripting a segment of a show which is composed of scenes edited to music? These notions are closer to necessity than absurdity. Have you ever seen a movie where people talked **all** the time?

Messages come across by the way people act, and not from what they say. Think of seeing a person's face as the person says, "No, I'm not nervous." Then pull back to see the person wringing his hands and crossing and un-crossing his legs as he continues, "Why should I be nervous about that?" Will you believe the person's words? Or his actions?

In the script for "Decision-Making", one of the Treatments you just read, there is a sequence in which four men are at their workplaces in the warehouse, but the fork lift operator appears to be dizzy. As the other people work, the fork lift operator becomes more and more uncontrolled until he finally wrecks the fork lift into the edge of shelving. Throughout this sequence there are sound effects, but not one spoken word.

Another program includes a segment on the process of packaging chemicals. It is a series of shots set to music, and again, there is not one spoken word. Yet in the script, there are seven scenes which describe what you see.

Try and use the visuals available to you in new and interesting ways. For example, a laser beam used to count particles in a liquid might be used to "dance" over other scenes.

In the finale of a show about products packaged in vials, hundreds of those vials could be placed in the shape of the company's logo. Weird-looking white "sterile" suits, used in the manufacturing process, could be used to create a scene of an all-white "home" environment, to show what it might be like to live in a sterile world. So, try, as much as you can, to let the pictures and sounds tell the story.

If you force yourself to become aware of the visuals already available as part of your topic's physical facilities, you will be able to find ways of using them as fascinating elements in your shows.

Another type of visual information relates strictly to locations. Many shows are boring because everything happens in the same place. If you look, you'll find plenty of locations for your actions to take place and you should include them in your script. Don't use a studio, except as a last resort. Go where the action **is**.

Even if you're tied to one place, you can still find other locations within it. Say, for example, you're working on a low-budget production and everything must be shot at a branch office. That office may still have within it: a reception area, bank of elevators, hallways, offices, open desk areas, and a vending machine area. Break up your story so that the action can take place in these different places.

Then, you must pay attention to what people **do**. Many shows are boring because in them, people just sit and talk. What other things might people do in conjunction with sitting and talking? Maybe they're near the vending machines, sitting and drinking coffee. What else? Someone takes a packet of sugar, puts the sugar in the coffee and stirs it. A simple thing, but simple things like that can help make the scene more realistic and visually interesting.

The same attention to detail should go into any kind of visual you script into your show: photographs, slides, cartoons, typography, graphics, animation, and so forth. Try to give enough description so that the person reading your script can imagine what this will look and feel like.

When you're writing, picture everything in your mind in detail and try to give as much information as possible in your script.

The Description

For each scene, you should describe where you are, whether it's an interior or an exterior, and the time of day if that's important.

You should try to avoid camera angles and jargon, but describe **what you see**. For example, you could describe a scene in a racketball court as, "Two men are playing racketball. One hits the ball, it bounces off the front wall and the other man races across the court, jumps up and just hits the ball, almost missing it." Or, you could describe what you see as, "A wooden floor. Two feet in yellow tennis shoes run past, then two feet in blue shoes run, stop, poise, jump up and disappear."

What you've done is described how the camera saw the scene, but without camera jargon. This is good because it focuses attention on the important elements of the scene and forces you to think about the details of what you really want to show. It also helps the client and other non-production people visualize what's going to be shot.

Sometimes you will read a script that's full of lingo like: pan here, CU, zoom there, MS, dolly past this, ELS, and so forth. When you read past the jargon, you realize that all you will see is a man sitting behind a desk in an office. Camera jargon is often nothing more than camouflage for a boring scene.

In Hollywood, a script full of technical terms is regarded as a sure sign of an amateur. So, forget the jargon and concentrate on describing what you want the scene to show.

Somewhere between VIDEO and AUDIO is a stage of contemplation which exemplifies what it is we are really doing — juxtaposing video and audio to create a message. You have the opportunity to create **new** meanings from visuals and sounds. By putting one thing with another, you will find that together the video and audio can mean something that neither means separately.

For instance, maybe you want to point out that working in an office can be as repetitive and mindless as working on an assembly line. You might show repetitive office actions, like stapling and copying, combined with repetitive sounds from a factory. The office actions alone don't signify factory work and the factory sounds alone don't relate to an office, but when you combine them, you create a new notion.

Or, perhaps you want to say that a choral program for underprivileged children influences their everyday lives. You might show the children singing in the choir, then continue the choir music as you show the children going about their daily routines in class, on the playground, and so forth. You have taken two things and combined them to create a new and memorable message, one that is different from what each element means as a separate entity.

The Audio

To think about the part audio plays in your work, consider popular songs. Have you ever had a favorite song, then one day read the lyrics on an album cover and were appalled? Did you discover that you hadn't the vaguest notion of what the lyrics were actually all about?

An audio visual program is somewhat like that. It's a total experience combining two elements. What people hear is totally integrated with what they see. Since the visuals are the stronger of the two elements, the audio isn't really meant to be thought of alone.

What kinds of audio do you have at your disposal? SILENCE, used effectively, can be very powerful. SPECIAL SOUND EFFECTS, like crashes and explosions, create a sense of drama. BACKGROUND SOUNDS add to reality. MUSIC has a diversity of uses. It can make transitions, fill the background, create rhythm, set a tone or build emotion.

You can enrich your show by using some combination of these sounds. Think about them and how they can complement each scene before you write any spoken words.

Natural sounds can be recorded on location. Sound effects and music can be originated, or, for a small fee, taken from audio libraries. If there is a popular song you like, you might ask the recording company for permission to use it, since yours is an in-house production and you're not selling the finished program.

If you can get your message across with the story your visuals tell, combined with sounds other than words, do it. For what you cannot otherwise reveal, use SPOKEN WORDS:

Dialogue. Dialogue should, above all, be a facsimile of people talking. People don't always converse in complete sentences; usually they don't. Learn to be a good listener and hear the people around you. Interview people and study their speech patterns. The only way you can copy anything is to be familiar with the original.

A dialogue is interaction, not a monologue. It should go back and forth. Design your information so that one person says something, then another person speaks.

You must create characters, preferably based on someone you know. Then, write for that person. Make each person's words fit his or her personality, and make sure you keep the character consistent throughout the show. As you write, you should act out the parts yourself, and see if they sound natural to you.

Interviews or Testimonials. Some shows are completely post-scripted; that is, scenes and interviews are shot, the show is edited together, then pieces of narration are scripted to tie everything together.

We are not talking about that kind of show here. We are concerned with **pre**-scripted shows, where you carefully design the show before production begins, so that you have control over each element.

You don't have much control if you simply interview someone, then select parts of that interview for your show. People tend to ramble; they take 50 seconds to say 12 seconds of worthwhile material. Without well-planned interviews, your ten-minute program can stretch itself into 30 minutes and the interview segments will be out of proportion with the rest of the show.

You can avoid this in one of two ways, each of which involves interviewing the person first. Bring an audio tape recorder, pencil and paper, and a list of questions. Then interview the person. Afterwards, you can do one of two things.

You can write a "script" for the person, using his or her own words, but in condensed form. Then videotape or film these remarks, using a teleprompter. With this method, people usually feel comfortable because they're saying their own words. If the person appears to be "reading", a few rehearsals should make it go more smoothly.

The alternative is to analyze what the person said in the initial interview and select the parts you want for your program. Make a list of questions which should elicit these specific responses (bring the page of hoped-for comments with you) and then interview the person on film or tape until you get the desired results.

Interview techniques will differ, depending on the person who is your subject. Your job is to make the person feel comfortable while you get the desired responses.

Narration. Over-written and poorly-written narration are often the downfall of in-house productions. Since nearly all shows will use narration in some form, it is essential to learn to write it well.

First of all, be short, sweet and simple. A good way to think about narration is to write it as though you were writing headlines — terse, rhythmic and memorable.

Narration does not have to be complete sentences, and probably shouldn't be. Think of phrases, phrases which merely add to what you are seeing, phrases which make you **feel** something about what you see.

Think about repeating phrases, like a refrain in a song. Think about writing "stanzas" with a certain rhythm, like a poem. Write spoken words, not written words. Make sure that the words you write sound good when they're said aloud.

You should avoid technical terms. Try to use simpler words, or define any technical ones you must use. Avoid tongue-twisters or alliterations, like "spectral slit-width spectrophotometers."

You should try to use the active voice and direct address, such as "turn the dial, then press the start button."

As a general rule, try not to let a sentence get any longer than 15 words. And try to have only one sentence per (10-second-or-so) scene.

Voice over narration is best written **after** the visuals are put together. This way, you can be certain that the words complement the video, and don't reiterate what you're seeing. However, in the video editing process, video and audio are usually edited simultaneously and thus the narration track must be pre-recorded.

After you write your spoken words, read them aloud. Maybe ask someone else to read them aloud. You might want to read them into a tape recorder, then play them back. You might hear something **you** didn't understand. You wrote those words. If you stumble over them, think of what a narrator will do as he or she reads them for the first time. And if they seem unintelligible to you, the audience will surely be confused.

Once you think you're finished writing a narration track, go over it again and try to take out 20 percent of the words. You just might be able to do it!

Then, everything should be read aloud again, to be certain that it's all simple and clear.

Review and keep in mind all of the basics, and all of the potentials of the video and audio, each time you begin a new script.

16
The Rough Script

It's been days, weeks, perhaps months since you first began working on this project. Now it's going to take its first step to becoming a reality: the Rough Script, or First Draft.

You shouldn't really think of it as "rough" or a "draft". Begin it as though it's the final script, and polish it as though it will be produced tomorrow. Unless you have that attitude, you may be lax, and your script's gems won't shine for their roughness. Besides, every once in a while — maybe the production deadline suddenly advances three weeks, or you're sent off on a trip somewhere — this **may** be used as the final script.

Before you begin, find your quiet place and get everything ready: your notes, Working Outline, Treatment, paper, pencils, eraser, typewriter, thesaurus, dictionary, stop watch, and anything else you might need. What you will do now is take your Treatment and translate it, as thoroughly as possible, into that blueprint for the production.

The first thing this Rough Script needs is a format. There are a number of commonly used formats, each of which you can explore.

The Formats

The Teleplay/Screenplay Format. The Writer's Guild of America calls this teleplay style "the accepted script format of the TV and motion picture industries." The WGA prints a booklet which gives a precise page layout, even so far as to indicate typewriter settings.

The Storyboard. These are used to help the client visualize something that you feel you cannot describe well enough with words. The storyboard is effective, but has one great pitfall — if you draw poorly and do not have an artist available to draw the scenes for you, your script may look unprofessional. It may end up more unintelligible than if you had tried to use words to describe your visuals.

The Split Page. This format is best used for slide show scripts. Many people do use this style for motion picture scripts, but it causes problems for a number of reasons. By its very style, it encourages the writer to script the spoken words first, which is exactly the opposite of what the writer should be doing.

SCRIPT FORMATS
Teleplay/Screenplay

```
FADE IN:

INTERIOR.  LUNCH PLACE WITH BOOTHS; BAR IN
BACKGROUND.  MEDIUM SHOT.

Four warehouse workers are sitting in booth.
JOE is a fork lift operator, in his mid-30's.
HANK is also a fork lift operator; he is an
older man.  They are with TWO PACKERS in
their early 20's.  All are wearing blue jeans
or other working clothes.  A few pitchers
of beer are on the table.  The men are
eating and drinking while they talk.
Juke box MUSIC is playing loudly in the
background.

                    JOE
          When's your daughter's
          wedding, Hank?

                    HANK
          Oh, another two weeks
          or so.

                    PACKER #1
          Hey, you gonna wear a tux?

Hank nods.
Packer #1 teases and pretends he's twisting the
corners of a bow tie.

                    PACKER #1
          Ho, ho!  I can't wait to see
          pictures of you in a ruffled
          shirt and bow tie ...

They all laugh.

                    HANK
          Keep talkin' like that
          and you won't be seein'
          anything.

Hank looks at the two packers.
```

Storyboard

<u>dissolve to:</u>

6. GRAPHICS/SIMPLE ANIMATION

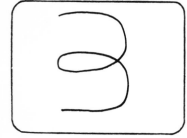

a) A copper-colored coil

NARRATOR: (VOICE OVER)

IT BEGINS WITH A
COPPER COIL.

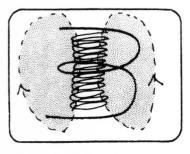

b) Lines moving in arcs
   outline a space enclosing
   red "magnetic fields".

MAGNETIC FIELDS
ARE GENERATED.

c) A spring-like column
   appears

AND THEN,
EDDY CURRENTS.

Split Page

<table>
<tr><td>VIDEO</td><td>AUDIO</td></tr>
</table>

VIDEO

SERIES OF SHOTS OF
RACING CAR ON ROADS:

1. Long shot of car speeding
   toward camera.

2. Subjective camera (from
   behind wheel) of going
   around curve.

3. Gloved hand
   shifting gears.

4. Car speeding over
   hill.

5. Gloved hand turning
   wheel.

6. Long shot of car travelling
   along road in an
   industrial-looking area.

7. Gloved hand
   shifting gears.

8. Car pulls up in front
   of Research Building
   Number 2.

AUDIO

SFX: VROOM VROOM OF ENGINE

MUSIC: EXCITING, FAST-PACED UP

MUSIC UP

MUSIC UNDER

NARRATOR:
(male-sophisticated with a touch
of a British accent)

SOME PEOPLE DEMAND

HIGH PERFORMANCE

IN EVERYTHING.

FROM THE AUTOMOBILES

THEY DRIVE ...

TO THE LABORATORIES

THEY RUN.

Corporate Teleplay

```
                                                 Page 4
cut to:

11. EXT. CHEMICAL MANUFACTURING DIVISION, (CITY).
    STAINLESS STEEL BRIDGE CONNECTING BUILDINGS
    ONE AND FOUR.

    a) NARRATOR is a man in his early 40's,
    dashing yet distinguished-looking, wearing
    a nice suit and an overcoat.  He walks across
    the bridge to the distillation pipe and
    sets his hand on the pipe.

              BACKGROUND SOUNDS UP AND UNDER

                  NARRATOR: (Lip Sync)

              What's the key to
              this specific purity?

    b) A close view of the fluid going through
    the pipe.

                  Distillation in
                  glass?

                  Yes.  But that's
                  not enough.

cut to:

12. GRAPHICS/SIMPLE ANIMATION.

    a) Graphic design of distillation arrangement,
    including flask, glass tubing and receptacle.
    Different-colored impurities (that look like grains
    of salt) move in the liquid.

                        NARRATOR: (VOICE OVER)


                  DISTILLATION IS THE

                  MOST VIABLE PROCESS

                  FOR REMOVING

                  IMPURITIES.
```

Almost worse than that is the problem this script creates with the client. For some reason, people have a tendency to read the AUDIO column first. If you've written the script correctly, letting the visuals tell the story with the spoken words supplemental, the audio will seem incomplete. The client often hastily concludes that the **script** is incomplete. Some people contend that if a script is written in a split page format, the client will never read the VIDEO portion at all.

Another problem with this format is that it doesn't look all that professional. Any person can write copy in this style. A teleplay format indicates a knowledgeable scriptwriter and hints to the client and others that it takes special skills to write a script.

In general, the biggest problem with the split page is that spoken words are not meant to stand alone as much as they appear to in this format.

The Corporate Teleplay Format. This corporate format is very similar to the WGA teleplay, except that it gives more attention to special things which must be considered with in-house productions.

The major differences in the corporate style are:

Scene Numbering. Specific scene numbers (1,2) and scene segments (a,b) are used for easy reference when discussing the script. It's easier to follow "Let's go back and check the wording on 2a" than "Go to the middle of the fifth page."

More Precise Locations. Instead of saying "A Small Library", an in-house script would say "The Fifth Avenue Branch of the City Library, 462 Fifth Ave. Reading Room, 2nd Floor." The main reason for doing this is that we usually know specific locations.

This extra effort on the writer's part helps the person doing the script breakdown to sort out all the locations. It also assures the client that you have chosen the correct place for that particular action.

Separate SFX and Music. Instead of being included in the scene description, Sound Effects (SFX) and MUSIC are placed in the middle column for quick reference and easy planning by the audio person.

Same Scene Descriptions. The descriptions are essentially the same — a full description of what will occur, with a minimum of camera movements and angles.

More Transitions. Transitions like cuts and dissolves are often specified, since they may be an element in the show's design. For example, if your equipment cannot make dissolves, the script must show how you plan to get from one scene to the next.

Same Dialogue Column. Lip-sync dialogue is still in a column in the center of the page, in both upper and lower case letters.

Separate Voice Over Column. Voice over narration is in a column on the right side of the page, all in upper case. The reason is that often the lip-sync portion is recorded on location, while the voice over part is done in a studio. This format separates the two, so that the director doesn't have to hunt through all of the copy to see which is voice over.

The Scene

The format you choose should be the one which will work best as a blueprint for your client and production team. When you have settled on a format, you can begin to write your Rough Script. Each scene in your script should include a number of basic things:

1. *The scene number,* as a reference for the client and production crew. Usually a location change triggers the change to a new scene.

2. *The precise location* of the action or a thorough description of the set you envision. If you're using photographs or artwork, specify and describe those.

Here, there are additional things to consider. If it's a photo in an album, will you show the edges to point out that it *is* a photo? Will you do camera moves on it? Where can the producer find these photos or artwork, or must they be created now?

This information is not only valuable, it's a necessity. Once the script is approved, it becomes the responsibility of the producer to produce these things, and if they are figments of your imagina-

tion with no back-up budget, you could become mighty unpopular.

3. *The talent.* Who do you see in this scene? Men? Women? How old are they? What do they look like? What are they wearing? Also, the first time a person's name appears in the script, the name is written in UPPER CASE to signify that this is a new character.

4. *The action.* What takes place in the beginning, during, and at the end of the scene? If there are people, describe in great detail what they are doing.

5. *The sound effects,* if any, should be included.

6. *The music,* if any, must be pointed out. Tell where it begins, ends, crescendos, and where it may be brought above or under other sounds.

7. *The spoken words.* Write the dialogue and narration.

8. *Any special props* you know about, like safety glasses or workman's outfits, should be enumerated.

The Producer's Scout

Very often, the budgets for non-broadcast shows aren't big enough for the producer or director to take a trip to scout the location. Often you, through your research, are the only one who's been there who had a chance to study the place with an eye and ear for shooting it.

Only **you** may know, for instance, that there are interesting sounds in the packaging department. If narration will be a voice over track recorded in the studio, maybe no one would record any location audio unless you specified that in your script.

And even though it may seem absurd, you should describe everything in extremely great detail. Why? Let's say you described an action in a scene as "Technician demonstrates blood coagulator." The producer would have no idea if that demonstration had three steps or thirteen, and if the shooting would take 45 minutes or four hours.

Multiply that by fifty scenes and three crew members with equipment, all on location, all on expense accounts. This difference comes to thousands of dollars.

The way you write your script **must** give the producer enough information to plan and budget the production. Remember that as you write.

Continue to write your Rough Script from your Treatment, translating your original design into scenes with precise actions, settings, sounds and spoken words.

Keep in mind that from your script, the producer should be able to:

- Coordinate locations or plan a set.
- Make a complete shot list.
- Choose the talent.

- Estimate with some precision that you're working within budget, and be able to do a fairly accurate budget breakdown.
- Know what props, sound effects and music will be needed.
- And, estimate shooting time and crew needed.

The client, on the other hand, should be able to read your script and know what to expect the finished show to look and feel like.

When you are through writing your Rough Script, re-read it thoughtfully. Read the audio aloud and time it. You may want to try and estimate times for segments without spoken words by acting the sequences out yourself. Tighten the script where you can.

If time permits, put the script away for a day or two, then go over it again with a fresh mind. Next, type it neatly and accurately, make the necessary copies, and put them in folders.

You can call it your Rough Script, but if you've written it well, there will only be minor revisions needed to smooth it into a Final Draft.

17
Presentation:
The Rough
Script Meeting

Your script now enters its most critical checkpoint stage.

A copy of the script should go to each of the technical advisors so they can check it for accuracy. When you send these copies, set a specific date for Comments/Revisions Due. Another script should go to the producer, and one to the director, so they can begin serious planning.

You can **send** the script to all of these people. But, if at all possible, you should present the script in person to the client. For, with the client, you must not only catch errors, you must catch implications. And, you must SELL the script.

Set up a meeting date with the client for what you can call the "Rough Script Meeting". It's a good idea to have the technical advisors' revised scripts back before this meeting, although that's not usually possible. It's also a good idea to invite the producer and director to this meeting. The client can get to know them, and they can help suggest changes if you run into snags.

Again, be professional. Make sure you bring enough copies of the script. Estimate how long you think the meeting will take to make certain that your client blocks out enough time and you won't be disturbed. One-and-a-half to two hours would be a good guess for a fairly complex 10-minute script. If you can, try to meet in a Conference Room, away from people's busy offices.

Bring all your notes and your Treatment to this meeting. If you have certain actors or actresses in mind, or a certain style or visual used in another program, bring photos or samples to show the client.

You should call your script the MASTER COPY. (Keep one clean copy separate for your files.) On this Master Copy, you will coordinate all changes from this meeting with the client, and those from technical advisors and the production people. You may want to put different peoples' comments in different-colored ink so you know who said what.

Acting Out the Script

From this meeting, you want the client to know how the show will look, feel and sound. Essentially, what you are to do is read the script. **You** should read the script aloud.

You can begin by re-stating your rationale for the treatment. Then, go over the script, scene by scene, describing fully every scene and reading the spoken words as you wish them to be heard. If your show happens to involve singing, dancing, or whatever — guess what else you should be prepared to do! If you're not an accomplished presenter, practice at home before the meeting.

What advantages do you have by presenting the script in person?

You can help the client understand what the show will actually be like. Since you **are** using words to describe pictures, sometimes even excellent scripts are hard to read. If you go through the script, describing, reading, and even drawing, the client should get the picture. You also have a chance to explain things more thoroughly.

Reading the script will make the audio come alive. By reading everything aloud, in the way you expect it to be heard, you will give the client an idea of the timing and the expressiveness. You will also avoid having to defend audio that sounds fine but doesn't read well. Dialogue is especially difficult for the client to "hear" from the page.

If there are changes to be made, *you* can make them. If you had sent the script to the client and he or she had made changes, it might be an affront to that person for you to re-word those words. This way, you're both content and you, the writer, are not put on the defensive.

You can bring up any questions you have in the back of your mind. Sometimes when you're writing the script, you realize you're missing some information, like how a process gets from D to F. If you were under a tight deadline or the person to ask was out of town, you might have logically "filled in the blank". Now's the time to ask if everything is correct.

This also forces you to write your script well. You have a lot more impetus to work and re-work your script when you know you'll have to read it aloud before this client audience.

The Selling of the Script

In reality, you are "selling" your script. You should be excited about it and you must get your client excited about it, too. Your main goal, after all, is to produce a script which will solve the client's problem. The client ought to think now that it will.

However, making sure of that is not always an easy task. You may discover that clients come in four categories, and you must be prepared to handle each.

First there are the Mad Tailors. These clients want to alter everything. To prepare for them, you need your Treatment, so they can be reminded that these elements had been approved. You should also defend things from a professional standpoint. You are the communications "expert" and you have reasons why you feel one thing works and another might not. If you let yourself be side-lined into awful changes, you can bet that these people will be the first to complain about what a lousy show you wrote.

Then, there are the YES-SAYERS. These clients will say yes and mean no. They are good-hearted and are often afraid to hurt your feelings. If you sense that some clients are afraid to make changes, probe those yesses. When the client seems uncomfortable about something, don't hesitate to say, "Do you think that's a good idea?" or "I did this for such and such a reason. Is that correct?" You want your client to be happy with this show. Clients will often have to watch the show many times, sometimes, even hundreds. Something with which they're unhappy will gnaw at them.

There was an instance where a voice over track about a product's label-counting machine said, "This is the same machine the U-S Treasury uses to count dollars." Well, of course, it wasn't **the** same machine, and it bothered that client every time he heard it.

You would also be amazed at the number of clients who have seen a show so many times (perhaps at a four-day conference, where it was continually re-run in booths where they had to stand) that they have the audio memorized. You had better think twice about making brash statements like "Everything in the universe is a chemical" or "Humans are the scale of all things" unless you believe that your client can live with that.

The third kind of clients are the SILENT ONES. These people do not trust their own judgements and will not admit to trusting yours. Force them to comment and give approvals now, or be prepared to face later changes and complaints which they will surely attribute to someone else.

Fourth are the RESPONSIVE ONES. These clients will take an interest in you and your work and will help you produce shows that will solve their problems. Appreciate them; they are a great part of what makes your job worthwhile.

So, be prepared to handle these clients and the complications, or lack of them, that arise at this meeting.

Always go through the script, scene by scene, word by word. Force yourself and your client to concentrate on every detail. If there are questions, explain what you've done, and why. Be open to criticisms and suggestions. Be flexible. Listen.

If, for some reason, there are unexpected major changes, like a sudden shift in a product's sales strategy, don't plan to proceed with a revised Rough Script. Instead, go back and write a new Treatment and get that approved first.

Make certain that you have decided how to handle every area in question before you leave this meeting and that all those notes are written on your master copy. Some things you may have re-written already, for others you may have simply written notes for changes you will re-write and have approved later.

After you and the client are satisfied with your discussions, you may want to leave and let the producer and director talk with the client about schedules. Usually they will know enough about the production to estimate the amount of work to be done and what cooperation they will need from the client and his or her associates.

The end result of this meeting should be SMILES— a feeling of optimism and cooperation and sounds of "It's gonna be a great one!"

18
Revisions to Final Script

Your master script will now have changes and notes from your Rough Script Meeting with the client. It may have notes for other changes suggested by the producer and director. And, by now you should have the changes from all the technical advisors and others to whom you sent a script.

If you happened to get back a script with no comments or changes, don't simply assume that you have already reached a level of perfection. Instead, suspect that the person never actually read the script, and give him or her a call. If any of these other changes are significant, check them with the client before incorporating them into your revisions. For minor changes, you can simply point them out to the client by encircling them on his or her copy of the revised script.

This script version, with all its notes and changes, becomes what is sometimes called the Pre-Production Draft. Go through this draft, page by page, making the revisions in what you expect to be their final form. See how the changes affect the script as a whole, and re-work as necessary.

The Final Script

When you are satisfied with all your revisions, type up the new version, which is sometimes called the Final Draft, Shooting Script, or Production Script.

It is helpful to the people who must approve the revisions if you identify the new material in your script. A simple method is to draw a vertical line in the right margin next to any changes. This way, they won't have to read the original version line for line to see what you've rewritten.

Make certain the new date is on there, too. Once again, send copies of the script to everyone involved. Ask for comments and revisions to be back by a certain date.

If there are yet further changes, be sure to either type a Revised Version of this script with a new date, or type only the revised pages and **personally** change them in everyone's script, or at least that of the client, producer and director.

From this point on, as the writer, you become a technical advisor to the production team. Maybe you will be asked to assist with the production, but usually you will act just as a consultant. If changes are requested, be understanding and flexible. All

sorts of unexpected things can happen with low-budget productions, from a role which must be shortened because an actor got the flu, to a major assembly line which breaks down the day your crew shows up.

Perhaps your show can't turn out exactly as you had written it. However, if it's a good script, and you have worked well with the production people up to this point, they will do their best to be true to your themes and will respect you enough to consult with you before making any major revisions. Learn to make compromises where necessary, and don't be offended by changes that other people make.

Save all your notes, tapes, Treatment, and copies of each version of the script, at least until the production is complete. It's a good idea to save everything for six months, just in case questions arise or for some reason a revised version of the finished show must be made. Sometimes, too, the Advertising Department may be working on a corollary promotion and your notes and ideas might be of value to them.

Now, you can rest. This is finally the time to set down your pencil on this show.

19
The Script as Dollars

The dollar value of the script is an issue which every writer should confront, even if you're a staff writer. Once you've had some good scripts through your typewriter, it's quite likely that you'll be asked to, or you'll want to, do free-lance work.

How much should you charge? How much is this script, and the work and time and experience it took to create it, worth? It's ever-changing, because every project, every client and every writer's talents are different. It is impossible to have a set rule or a set price.

Here, then, are a number of methods that different writers use:

1. The price-per-finished-minute charge
2. The percent-of-budget offer
3. The up-front bid
4. The pay-in-three-parts contract
5. The post-charge
6. The flat-fee-plus-residuals charge

These are meant to be a sampling, and not an all-inclusive list. The method or methods you use will be up to you. Take a look at each of these, examining what they entail and their pros and cons.

1. The Price-Per-Finished-Minute Charge.
Some people charge a dollar-per-finished-minute-of-show rate, which may be anywhere from $25 to $150 or more. The question is whether this can elicit a fair price for your work. Your best scripts may be (and probably should be) the briefest, but the most complex. These are scripts which take a lot of research and material, honed down to a compact frame, then developed and polished into an exciting experience.

With a price-per-finished-minute, you are tempted to write long shows, which are the most boring and the most deadly to your reputation. If you write a wonderfully brief show, you may have to charge what seems like an outrageous amount per minute, or you could end up working for a pittance. This, as with all the other methods, is yours to consider.

2. The Percent-of-Budget Offer.
In this instance, someone will offer you, as the scriptwriter, a percentage of the show's total budget, usually 10 percent. This seems fair enough. So, if the show has a high budget, you're all set. But what if the show has an average or low budget? Then, you must consider whether you think you will be paid enough for the work you will have to do.

This sort of proposal, unless you are famous and have a bargaining edge, will usually be a "take it or leave it" offer. You must know how to judge whether or not it will be a good one.

3. *The Up-Front Bid.* This is probably what you will be asked to do most often, so you must be prepared and not just stutter, "Um . . . gee, I don't know . . . "

The first thing you must do is estimate how much time this project will take. If you don't have a really good idea of how much time you've spent on other shows you've done, you're in trouble. You should get into the habit of keeping track of all the hours you spend on each job. At the end of every day or the beginning of the next day, add up (to the quarter-hour if you can) the time you spent working on each scriptwriting project.

Some writers differentiate the "kinds" of hours and have rates accordingly. This might be: "light" time, for travelling or doing clerical-type work; "medium" time, such as reading material or sitting in meetings; and "intense" time, in solitary concentration and writing.

It can be said, "My time is my time." That is true, but you may spend a lot of light hours on a job and then charge a preposterous amount for it. On the other hand, you may spend a short time with much more intense work to create a very astounding finished show. Unless you consider these things, you may short-change yourself or bid yourself out of the ballpark.

TIME AND EXPENSE-KEEPING

JOB TITLE:

NUMBER:

TIME

DATE	MEETING	RESEARCH	WRITING	MISC

EXPENSES:

MEALS

DATE	WITH WHOM	AMT

LODGING

DATE	WHERE	AMT

TRANSPORTATION

DATE	WHERE	mlg/pkg

LONG DISTANCE CALLS

DATE	TO WHOM	AMT

COPYING/MISCELLANEOUS

DATE	WHAT	AMT

SUB-TOTAL

x $/hour

TOTAL

EXPENSES SUB-TOTAL $ _____

=   =   =   = $ _____

TOTAL $ _____

Even though no two scripts will be alike, if you keep track of your time, you will be able to see patterns emerge which will help you estimate your time. To give an up-front bid, try to find out: how many people you will have to interview, how many places you will have to visit and how long that will take, how much reading and other research you will have to do, and how many people will have to approve this script.

Once you've estimated what your total hours might be on the project, multiply them by what you've determined to be the appropriate hourly rate, and there you have your bid. Some people recommend adding 25 percent, just to make certain you've covered yourself. Next, type up your bid and make a copy for yourself.

Your bid should explicitly state what it includes, and often what it **doesn't** include, like "plus expenses". So, if the client asks you to do something you hadn't planned, like attend the shooting or editing sessions, you can remind him or her that that wasn't included in the bid and renegotiate an added fee.

Experience helps you to manage better, but you will always be guessing. With the up-front bid, one of three things will have happened to you: a) You under-guessed, and found that you worked for $2 an hour. b) You over-guessed, and depending on your personality, either feel guilty or smug. c) You guessed right on the button, but still had to work under the onus of clock-watching your creative thinking.

Clients usually feel most comfortable with this up-front method, because they know exactly what to expect. The problem is, **you** don't.

4. The Pay-in-Three-Parts Contract. Some writers ask for a three-part contract. This is an up-front bid, with one-third paid in advance, one-third paid at a certain stage, like the first draft of the script, and one-third paid upon completion.

This is great when projects require a great deal of up-front travelling and payment for research, or when projects will extend over a long period of time. Its disadvantage is the same as the bid. You are tied to a specific dollar amount, which often cannot be changed with the discovery that you must do much more work than anticipated.

5. The Post-Charge. This is, perhaps, the fairest method, because the client is paying for, and you are being paid for, all the work that was actually done. This is an especially good method when you are working on a project of an unusual nature, when you don't know what to expect.

However, unless clients know you and trust you (and even if they do), it is difficult for them to give you a job and not know what the script will cost and how that will fit into the show's budget.

If you have a demo tape with a number of different shows on it, you could say, "This show was this much, a kind like this would be this much" and so on. You also may be able to give a rough estimate, like "This will be between $1200 and $1500;

no more than that" and then it might be acceptable for you to charge the actual fee.

6. The Flat-Fee-Plus-Residuals. This may happen when the project is one which the client intends to sell, and, as with all the other fee methods, may or may not be to your advantage. The flat fee will usually result in a lower payment for the script, but with the potential for making a profit in residuals. You may want to explore this company and its past endeavors, and question yourself as to how much of a gambler you are.

Getting Your Money

Beware of speculative projects. Unless you are really anxious to get a particular client or work on a particular project (and even then, it's dubious), don't work for less than you're worth or for nothing. It reduces the value of your work, it's not very good for your self-image, and it will most likely cause problems when you try to charge for work later.

Before you do any work, make certain it's clear and agreed upon, preferably in writing, what services you will provide and what the financial arrangements will be. It's uncomfortable to some people, but even so, don't be afraid to talk about money.

Bill a job as soon as you are certain that the final script has been approved. If you are not paid after a month, call. If it seems as though it's taking a long time, be firm and persistent about getting

INVOICES

An invoice composed on your business stationery.
Keep a copy for your records.

```
Donna Matrazzo
Scripts and Concepts

The Westbury #1101
271 South 15th Street
Philadelphia, PA 19102
(215) 545-2896


                              INVOICE


TO:  Client, The Blank Company

INVOICE NO.: 8-117-11

CLIENT JOB NO.: BC 189

DATE:


DESCRIPTION                            AMOUNT

First half of Script Fee
upon completion of                   $1,000.00
Treatment for videotape program,
"Yesterday and Tomorrow"

Treatment accepted
(date)


EXPENSES

Travel (date)                            50.00

Meals (date)                             20.00
                                     ----------

TOTAL                                $1,070.00
```

A three-part form which can be inexpensively printed.
One form is for your records;
2 forms go to the client, one will be returned with payment.

```
Donna Matrazzo          To      Client
                                The Blank Company
                        Invoice No   8-117-11
The Westbury #1101
271 South 15th Street   Client Job No  BC 189
Philadelphia, PA 19102
(215) 545-2896          Date      (date)

Amount                  Description

$2,000.00               Research
                        Script Treatment
                        Rough Script and
                        Final Script for videotape program

                        "Yesterday and Tomorrow"

                        Final Script accepted
                        (date)
```

your money. If you've decided that this client doesn't intend to pay, there's always the Small Claims Court.

When it comes to turning your scripts into dollars, what is right? Keep in mind that what a script is worth is a combination of factors, weighted in different ways:

- Your time
- The complexity of the topic and the project
- The intensity of your creative efforts
- Your years of experience
- How good your past scripts have been, often proven by awards
- Recommendations from others
- What your competition is charging

What **is** right? The most important thing is to do the best work possible. Then, charge what **you** honestly think your work is worth.

20
Script Evaluation

Writers usually have a good idea of whether or not their scripts are terrific, but often don't know why. People who must hire writers or who must approve scripts are often faced with the same dilemma.

So many different people look for so many different things from a script, it's difficult to say which things are the most important. How **can** scripts be evaluated? Here is a proposed method, or set of questions, which looks at the script on three general levels: Effectiveness, Creativity, and Craftsmanship.

Effectiveness

Ask yourself:

Will this script solve the client's problem?

Will it elicit the desired emotional response from the audience?

Does it get the message across clearly?

Does it accomplish what was stated as the show's purpose?

Does it include everything that's essential?

Do you feel that it was thoroughly researched, or does the material seem shallow and merely touching the surface of the topic?

Do you feel confident about your judgement in choosing the way the topic is portrayed?

Does it seem complete? Is it well-developed, telling its story fully, without gaps or taking people down "side alleys"?

Do you think its length is right for its message?

Creativity

Will the audience enjoy it? Will they want to keep watching it? Will they appreciate it? Will they identify with it?

Is it interesting? Or, is it just a jumble of information held together by an audio visual format?

Do the concept and content work together throughout?

Is it still the best way you can imagine to present the subject?

Was there an effort to make each element of the show as interesting as possible? Or, were some parts highly imaginative and others dull?

Does the script show a proper use of the production capabilities available? Does it utilize your resources of equipment, talent, sounds, music, graphics, etc. appropriately?

Will it make the production people excited to be working on this show? Will they be proud of it?

Craftsmanship

Is this script skillfully written with a knowledge of scriptwriting and production techniques?

Does it give an accurate idea of what you expect the final production to look like?

Does it contain all the information which you are able to give the production staff?

Is it fully visualized? Can **you** picture every scene?

Are the dialogue and narration well-written?

Are all the segments well integrated?

More Questions

After reading the script, you can ask yourself three big questions:

Could someone else, immediately after reading this script, talk comfortably about the subject?

Creatively speaking, could it win an award?

If you handed this script to a producer, could he or she plan the production completely from what's written on those pages?

Each of these areas is, of course, integrated with the others. For example, how can a script be effective if it's not interesting? These questions are merely to help you evaluate your script in terms of its strengths and weaknesses, and what other people are demanding of you. Your script's true assessment, after all, is determined by how good the finished production is and whether or not it solved the client's problem.

An added measure of self-evaluation is to look at the finished show and compare it, scene for scene and word for word, with the final version of your script. You will see where the director had to add another scene because you didn't include a good transition. You will wince as you see the on-camera narrator, on camera far too long. And you might see a scene which looks very different from what you had envisioned, then realize you wrote it the way it was shot.

The most important aspect of evaluation is recognizing that you must do it. Force yourself to always evaluate scripts, both your own and others. What you really want is to make each script as good as you can. Then learn from it to make the next one better.

21
Conclusion

This conclusion is, of course, still just the beginning. The notions that have been put forth are not hard and fast rules; there are none. Just as there are no pre-conceived solutions to all the problems you will face. And no guarantees of success.

These are merely the essentials, the hows, whys and wherefores of the creation of a script. Knowing how to draw a blueprint doesn't mean you can design a cathedral. So, knowing how to write a script doesn't mean you will instantly produce masterpieces. But you need to know the basics before you can go on to do anything great. The potential, and the promise, are yours.

As with anything worthwhile, scriptwriting is a lot of hard work, but with its rewards. There will be grimaces, applause, long hours, notes of thanks, endless cups of coffee, well-earned awards, bleak days, brilliant days, and lasting frustrations and exultations.

The results are creations that are truly YOU. No one, now or ever, would have created exactly the same script. No one would ever have treated that subject in exactly the same way, designed the same scenes, phrased the same words.

The results are a reflection of you, your beliefs, your experiences, your talents, your dedication and your very living. A script is no small thing.

And what you have created is something most valuable. It is a program that will be viewed and viewed, perhaps for years, perhaps by tens of thousands of people. You are teaching them, communicating with them, persuading them, informing them, motivating them. You touch many minds and hearts. On the scale of all the things that you could have done with your time and your mind, a script is no small thing.

You respond to people's responses, and grow yourself. And as with anything else that is rewarding, you derive from it what you put into it.

> Write with wonder.
> Write with optimism.
> Write with emotion.
> Write with understanding.
> Write with wisdom.
> Write to please yourself, and to give pleasure to others.

Your rewards can only multiply.

Appendix

I have included two complete scripts in this book. You have already read the Treatments for both; now you can follow through the development into finished scripts.

I chose these two because they exemplify almost two extremes of corporate scripts. The first is a relatively simple tale illustrating the five-step decision-making process. The second is much more complex, with its many different aspects loosely tied together with a concept.

"Decision-Making"

This program is part of a Management Training series. These shows are viewed by ten to fifteen supervisors in a Training Session, led by a discussion leader and accompanied by a printed Leader's Guide and Participant's Manual.

"Decision-Making" was designed to impart information about the process and to instigate discussion among the supervisors.

The series itself has been very successful; I chose this particular script for a number of reasons:

It is a drama, so this is a case of an entertainment parody which turned out well.

The story is based on information derived from research and adapted to this writer's experiences. The client had told me a few stories of "drunk" people who had been fired by supervisors who hadn't bothered to find out the facts. I made the person a diabetic, since my mother is a diabetic and I am very familiar with insulin shock.

The script shows an opening scene that was not written in the treatment. The producer/director suggested adding the "bar" scene to give a twist to the program. By showing the fork lift operator in a liquor-drinking situation, we set up the audience to make a wrong snap judgement. So, you can see how collaboration improved the script.

Discussion Breaks were woven into the fabric of the story.

Voice over narration was kept to a minimum. Much of the information which might normally be written as voice over was designed as a fast-paced and thought-provoking dialogue between the Foreman and the Operations Manager.

We found excellent local actors.

All of these factors combined to help this show become a success.

"The Truck Builders"

I chose this program, in part, because it's an employee orientation show. More than likely, you'll have to do such a program at some time in your corporate scriptwriting career.

It's also quite typical of corporate programming in general — a show with a great many elements that must be included and tied together imaginatively and cohesively.

The voice over narration here is succinct and nicely polished.

The completed videotape, which followed this script very closely, won awards from the International Film and TV Festival of New York, the ITVA International Awards Festival and the JVC Business & Industry Videotape Festival.

Notes

Originally, my plans were to include two **perfect** scripts here. As I hunted through my work for these masterpieces, I realized that not only do I not have any scripts I consider "perfect" — I'm not sure I even know what a perfect script is.

I can spot flaws in every script; as you read these, you probably will, too. You'll say, "I thought that part seemed muddled" or "Aha, look, here's some camera jargon!" What can I say?

I think what's important is to write every script to the best of your ability so that it does its job, and then try and learn from it.

What makes me feel good about an old script, and my work? I am pleased when I can look at a show in times hence and still feel with pride an "Oh, Wow!" over some parts — yet look at other parts, groan, turn to the person sitting next to me and teasingly comment, "Did I write that?!"

SCRIPT
"Decision-Making"

Donna Matrazzo
Scripts and Concepts

The Westbury #1101
271 South 15th Street
Philadelphia, PA 19102
(215) 545-2896

"DECISION-MAKING"

FINAL SCRIPT

(Date)

"Decision-Making"

PURPOSE: To teach viewers the basic steps involved
in the decision-making process:
Getting the facts
Verifying them
Identifying the real problem
Finding possible solutions
Deciding upon a solution

To instigate discussion on the facets
of decision-making.

AUDIENCE: All company supervisors (office and plant)

REQUESTED BY: (Client's name, number and location)

TECHNICAL ADVISORS: (Advisors' names, numbers and
locations)

PRODUCER:

DIRECTOR:

WRITER:

STATUS:

Script Treatment:

Rough Script:

Production Planning Meeting:

Final Script:

Shooting Dates:

Final Edit:

Copies for Distribution:

"Decision-Making"

<u>Decision-Making</u>

<u>FADE IN</u>:

1. TITLE. USUAL ANIMATION SEQUENCE FOR THIS
   SUPERVISORY SERIES.
   <u>SUPER</u>: DECISION-MAKING.

FADE OUT

<u>FADE IN</u>:

2. INT. LUNCH PLACE WITH BOOTHS, BAR IN BACKGROUND.
   (PROBABLY SOUPER BOWL OR FRANK & WALLY'S)

   a) Four warehouse workers are sitting in a booth.
   JOE, fork lift operator, mid-30's; HANK, fork
   lift operator, older man; and TWO PACKERS, early
   20's. They are wearing jeans or other working
   clothes. A few pitchers of beer are on the
   table. The men are eating and drinking while
   they talk.

   <u>NATURAL SOUNDS</u>

   <u>MUSIC</u>: LOUD DISCO MUSIC
   <u>FROM</u> JUKE BOX.

      Joe:
   When's your daughter's
   wedding, Hank?

      Hank:
   Oh, another two weeks
   or so.

      Packer #1:
   Hey, you gonna wear
   a tux?

   b) Hank nods. Packer #1 teasingly pretends that
   he's twisting the corners of a bow tie.

      Packer #1:
   Ho, ho! I can't wait to see
   <u>you</u> in a ruffled shirt and
   <u>bow</u> tie ...

"Decision-Making"

c) They all laugh.

>   Hank:
>   You keep talkin' like that
>   and you won't see anything!

d) He looks at the two packers.

>   Just wait'll you have kids.

e) He looks at Joe.

>   <u>You</u> have kids, don't you,
>   <u>Joe</u>?

f) Joe takes a drink from his glass.

>   Joe:
>   Yeah, no girls, though.
>   Three boys.

>   Packer #2:
>   Hey, doesn't one of them play
>   Little League with my nephew?

g) Joe points with his glass.

>   Joe:
>   That's the oldest. That's
>   right, we saw you at the field.

>   Hank:
>   ... Little League! ... Wait'll
>   I have a grandson ...

>   Packer #1:
>   (Waiting for a chance to act
>   rowdy) A <u>grandson</u> already ...
>   listen to <u>him</u> ...

h) Packer #2 laughs and raises his glass.

>   Packer #2:
>   That's okay ... C'mon, let's make
>   a toast ... to a grandson for
>   Hank...

i) They all raise glasses in a toast and clink them
together, then drink. Joe's glass has iced tea, but
it looks like a mixed drink. It's different from
all the others, which are beer glasses.

>   All:
>   Hear, hear! Yeah! etc.

"Decision-Making"

dissolve to:

3. EXT. STREET OUTSIDE LUNCH PLACE.

   The four men come out of the door of the restaurant
   and walk together down the street. They are
   laughing and carrying on -- shoving each other
   lightly, making faces, etc.

   NATURAL SOUNDS

dissolve to:

(NOTE: Scenes 4 through 9 should give a feeling of
time passing. Each time we see Joe, he looks a little
more unsteady.)

4. INT. BRANCH. WAREHOUSE AREA.

   The four men go back to their work stations; they
   are all in a good mood. The two packers go to
   their packing areas, look at the order write-ups
   and begin taking boxes to pack. Joe and Hank go
   to their fork lifts and start them up.

   NATURAL SOUNDS

Series of cuts of these people at work:

5. PACKING STATION. Packer #1 fills a box with
   tamping material.

6. AISLE. Rear view as Joe drives fork lift down an
   aisle. He stops it, then starts it again slowly.

7. REVERSE ANGLE of fork lift. Joe's face looks
   glassy-eyed and drowsy.

8. PACKING STATION. Packer #2 carries a wrapped
   and labelled box to the conveyer belt.

9. AISLE. Joe's fork lift weaves down an aisle,
   turns and smashes into the corner of shelving.
   Some boxes fall from the shelf onto the floor,
   a few bottles break and the contents spill.

   SFX: CRASH, GLASS BREAKING

   FOOTSTEPS OF PEOPLE RUNNING

"Decision-Making"

> Off-camera voices: (overlapping)
> Hey, what's happening?...
> Everything okay over there?...
> What's goin' on?...

cut to:

10. INT. WAREHOUSE. A DIFFERENT AISLE.

a) WAREHOUSE FOREMAN, TOM BAILEY (30's wearing
slacks, open-collared shirt) runs down the aisle,
turns the corner and stops as he spots the
accident. Hank, the other fork lift operator,
is stopped there with his machine. Tom turns
to him and they both hurry down the aisle.

> Tom:
> What's going on, Hank?

> Hank:
> I dunno. I saw Joe
> weavin' back 'n forth,
> like he was ...

b) Hank stops, catches himself. Tom stops and
looks at him with a cold stare.

> ... like he was dizzy.
> And then ...

11. INT. WAREHOUSE. AISLE FROM SCENE 9.

a) Follow Tom and Hank around the corner to this
aisle. The two packers are holding up Joe, who
can barely stand. Tom approaches and Joe slowly
breaks into a silly, smirking grin and teasingly
moves his eyebrows up and down. The two packers
look at him nervously. Tom approaches and studies
him.

> Tom:
> You okay, Conley?

b) Joe shakes his head slowly up and down,
still grinning.

> Joe:
> Shu-ure. Ah'm just dan-dy ...

"Decision-Making"

c) The two packers look at each other. Tom
looks at them.

> Tom:
> You're dandy all right!

d) Tom notices the bottles spilled on the floor.

> Oh, no! That's <u>hydrochloric
> acid</u>!

e) Tom looks around to make sure everyone's okay.

> We don't need this ...
> You're fired!
> Can one of you guys take
> him home?

f) The two packers look at each other. Packer #2
shakes his head.

> Packer #2:
> Yeah, I can.

> Tom:
> Well, get him out of here.
> The rest of you ... Let's see
> if we can get this cleaned
> up ... Be careful ...

g) The two packers lead Joe away. He's still
grinning and he turns his head back and forth
between them. Tom is standing there shaking his
head.

<u>dissolve to:</u>

12. INT. OPERATIONS MANAGER'S OFFICE.
(A small, plain cubicle in the warehouse)

a) Tom pokes his head in the doorway. The OPERATIONS
MANAGER, AL HERMAN (early 50's, wearing shirt
and tie) is seated behind the desk. He looks up.

> Tom:
> Got a minute, Al?

> Al:
> Sure, Tom. C'mon in.
> Have a problem?

"Decision-Making"

b) Tom comes into the office and sits down.

> Tom:
> I'm not sure what to call it.
> Y'know our new guy ... Conley...

> Al:
> Fork lift operator, isn't he?

c) Tom nods his head.

> Tom:
> Yep. In fact, his 90 days were
> almost up. Seemed like a good
> guy.

d) Tom starts to rub his chin.

> Then, about an hour ago, he
> was drunk as a skunk and drove
> the lift into some shelves.
> Smashed up the lift ... Knocked
> over a bunch of H-C-L-2.

e) Al sits up in his seat.

> Al:
> HCL-2! Anybody hurt?

f) Tom shakes his head.

> Tom:
> No, but that was sheer luck.
> Anyway, he was grinning like a
> fool ... couldn't stand up ...
> and I lost my head and
> fired him on the spot.

> Al:
> And what do you think you
> should do now?

g) Tom leans back in his seat and shrugs his
shoulders.

> ANNOUNCER VOICE OVER:
>
> YOU ARE TOM BAILEY, THE
>
> FOREMAN. THE ACTION
>
> YOU HAVE JUST TAKEN
>
> MAY SEEM LIKE A CLEAR-
>
> CUT DECISION.

"Decision-Making"

Page 7

ANNOUNCER VOICE OVER:

BUT, IN FACT, YOU HAVE

NOT EVEN BEGUN THE

REAL DECISION-MAKING

PROCESS. WHAT SHOULD

YOU DO NOW?

cut to:

13. ARTWORK: USUAL "DISCUSSION BREAK" ART FOR THIS
    SERIES.

STOP THE TAPE AND

DISCUSS YOUR PLAN OF

ACTION.

FADE OUT

FADE IN:

14. INT. OPERATIONS MANAGER'S OFFICE. (Same as Scene 12)

    a) Al, the Operations Manager, is seated behind his
    desk. Tom is sitting opposite him in a chair.
    Al looks up from some notes.

                    Al:
              So, you're telling me this
              is the situation: Joe Conley,
              the new fork lift operator,
              ran the lift into some
              shelves, and you fired
              him.

                    Tom:
              Yes, but I fired him because
              he was drunk, not because
              he ran into the shelves.

                    Al:
              Why do you say he was
              drunk?

                    Tom:
              Well, he could hardly
              stand up ... and he was
              slurring his words ...
                    (continued)

"Decision-Making"

> Tom:
> and he just <u>looked</u> drunk.
> You know, his <u>face</u> and all.

> Al:
> Did you smell liquor on
> his breath?

b) Tom scratches his head.

> Tom:
> Hmmm. Not that I remember.
> But the guys on the floor
> said he was weaving back
> and forth down the aisle.

c) Al looks back at his notes.

> Al:
> You said his first 90 days were
> almost up. Have you had any
> problems with him before?

> Tom:
> Not really. Although now
> a few of the guys say he
> acted funny sometimes.

d) Al leans over his desk toward Tom.

> Al:
> What do you think they
> meant, "acted funny"?

> Tom:
> Oh, that he sort of acted as
> though his mind were someplace
> else. Glassy-eyed, maybe.

> Al:
> Do you think they meant
> "drinking"?

> Tom:
> I guess. I don't know.

e) Al sits back in his chair.

> Al:
> Back to today. Did
> anybody <u>see</u> him drinking?

"Decision-Making"

f) Tom shakes his head.

>   Tom:
>   Oh...my fault. I should've
>   mentioned this right up
>   front: The guys were over
>   the Keg 'n Kettle for lunch.
>   Went through a couple
>   pitchers of beer, I
>   understand.
>
>   Al:
>   Beer, huh?

g) Tom tightens his lips.

>   Tom:
>   Yeah. I guess I ought to
>   ask around and see if
>   anyone noticed how much
>   he had to drink.
>
>   Al:
>   That's a good idea. And
>   what about his record? Do
>   you remember anything about
>   his other job? If he'd had
>   any trouble before?
>
>   Tom:
>   I can't remember. But I
>   would've noticed something
>   like that when I hired him.
>   I'll check, though. I'd like
>   to talk to the other guys
>   some more, too.
>
>   Al:
>   And what about talking to
>   Conley?

h) Tom slowly shakes his head.

>   Tom:
>   Yeah, that's a tough one
>   right now. I think I need
>   to find out as much as I
>   can here before I call him.
>
>   Al:
>   Okay, why don't you do that, then.
>   How long do you think it
>   will take?

"Decision-Making"

i) Tom begins to get up.

> Tom:
> Oh, a day or two.

j) Al looks at his calendar.

> Al:
> Then how about getting
> back to me Friday?

k) Tom is exiting out the doorway.

> Tom:
> Sounds fine.

> Al:
> All right. I'll see you then.

dissolve to:

15. INT. TOM'S WORK AREA.
     (A corner with a desk and file cabinet)

     Tom goes into the file cabinet and pulls out a
     folder, then sits down behind his desk. He
     flips through the papers, reading some of the
     information.

                    NATURAL SOUNDS

cut to:

16. INT. WAREHOUSE. AISLE.

     Tom is talking to Hank, who is on his fork lift.

> Hank:
> Sure, we were all
> drinking beer.

cut to:

17. INT. WAREHOUSE. PACKING AREA.

     Tom is with Packer #1, who is tamping a box.

> Packer #1:
> He told me he never touches
> a drop. Come to think of it,
> he ordered apple juice, or
> something wierd.

"Decision-Making"

Page 11

cut to:

18. INT. PERSONNEL OFFICE. DESK/FILE CABINET AREA.

Tom is standing next to a file cabinet, looking
through a stack of computer printout sheets.

cut to:

19. INT. WAREHOUSE. PACKING AREA.

Tom is with Packer #2 (The packer who drove Joe home).

> Packer #2:
> Nope, didn't say a word the
> whole trip. Got there, his
> wife looked real scared. I
> helped him into the house.
> She said he'd be fine. I
> can take a hint, so I left.

cut to:

20. INT. WAREHOUSE. AISLE.

Tom is talking with Hank, who is stepping down
from his fork lift.

> Hank:
> Y'know, it seemed like he was
> always eating something while
> he worked ...

cut to:

21. INT. HALLWAY.

Follow as Tom walks down the hallway, carrying
a file folder and a book.

> MUSIC: DRAMATIC AND BUILDING

cut to:

22. INT. OPERATIONS MANAGER'S OFFICE.

a) Al is seated behind his desk. Tom walks in,
grim-faced, and comes beside Al, who is silently
watching him. Tom pulls out a company MEDICAL
RECORDS sheet from the folder and points to the
word "Diabetes" with a check mark beside it.

> MUSIC UNDER

"Decision-Making"

b) Tom places the opened book on top of the
sheet. It's a Medical Book. He points to a
paragraph under "Diabetes" which reads "... an
insulin-shock reaction takes on the appearance
of intoxication."

MUSIC CRESCENDO AND OUT

Al:
(He looks to Tom)
And now, what?

c) They both look back down and begin to pick
up the other papers in the folder and look at
them.

ANNOUNCER VOICE OVER:

YOU ARE TOM BAILEY, THE

FOREMAN. YOU'VE

GATHERED THE FACTS.

YOU HAVE WHAT YOU BE-

LIEVE ARE THE TRUE FACTS.

WHAT DO YOU THINK ABOUT

THE SITUATION NOW?

WHAT IS THE REAL

PROBLEM?

cut to:

23. ARTWORK: DISCUSSION BREAK.

STOP THE TAPE AND

DISCUSS THE NEXT

ACTIONS YOU WOULD TAKE.

FADE OUT

FADE IN:

24. INT. OPERATIONS MANAGER'S OFFICE.

a) Al is seated behind his desk. Tom takes the
seat opposite him.

"Decision-Making"

                    Al:
                    So, things aren't always
                    what they seem.

b) Tom settles back in the chair.

                    Tom:
                    I guess they hardly ever are.

c) Al points to the file folder.

                    Al:
                    But now you have all your
                    answers ... yes?

                    Tom:
                    Hmmph. Not only do I <u>not</u>
                    have the answers ... Now I
                    have a different problem.

                    Al:
                    Yes?

d) Tom leans forward across Al's desk.

                    Tom:
                    Tuesday, my problem was an
                    accident and how to prevent
                    others and how to get things
                    back to normal. I thought I
                    solved all that by firing Joe.

e) Al picks up a pipe on his desk.

                    Al:
                    And now?

f) Tom plops back in the chair and crosses his arms.

                    Tom:
                    Now, instead of worrying about
                    the accident ... I'm worrying
                    about Joe.

                    Al:
                    What do you think you should do?

                    Tom:
                    I'm not sure. On the one hand,
                    his was a medical problem, so
                    he <u>wasn't</u> drunk. But ...

"Decision-Making"

g) Al taps the bowl of his pipe against an ashtray.

> Al:
> Go on ...

h) Tom uncrosses his arms.

> Tom:
> But it was his fault. He
> knew that something like this
> could happen with his diabetes.
> And he could've really hurt
> someone.

> Al:
> What do you think might
> be a solution?

i) Tom shakes his head.

> Tom:
> I don't know yet. I'll have
> to talk to him and a lot will
> depend on what he has to say.
> I can't give him that job
> back, that's for sure.

j) Al puts some tobacco into his pipe.

> Al:
> What would you like to do?
> And how do you feel about
> him now.

k) Tom breaks into a half-smile, then rubs his chin.

> Tom:
> I have to admit, after I saw
> that on his medical record, I
> started to remember all the things
> I like about Joe ... and why
> I hired him in the first place.
> But, to answer your first
> question ... I don't know
> what else I can do with him.
> I have to see how he feels.

> Al:
> Do you think he'd like to
> come back?

"Decision-Making"

> Tom:
> Who knows? Then there would
> have to be another job and
> we don't have anything else
> open.

1) Al lights his pipe and takes a few puffs.

> Al:
> What about in another department?

> Tom:
> Could be. A lot will depend on
> how often he has these things.

> Al:
> What are your plans now?

m) Tom begins to gather the papers.

> Tom:
> I'm going to ask him to
> come in and have a talk.

n) Al nods his head and sets the pipe in the
ashtray.

> Al:
> Fine. Keep me posted. How
> about stopping in next Wednesday?

o) Tom picks up the folder and the book.

> Tom:
> Sounds good.

FADE OUT

FADE IN:

25. EXT. BRANCH PARKING LOT. (LOWER LOT, RIDGE AVE.)

Tom and Joe walk across the lot and get in a car.

NATURAL SOUNDS

> Tom:
> We'll just get a cup of
> coffee ... Get away from all
> that while we talk ...

"Decision-Making"

dissolve to:

26. INT. COFFEE SHOP. (2ND FLOOR CAFETERIA OR DIFFERENT
    SECTION OF THE SOUPER BOWL)

    a) Tom and Joe are seated at a small table.
    Each has a cup of coffee.

                    NATURAL SOUNDS

    b) Joe is looking down at his cup.

                    Joe:
                    I'm sorry, Tom ... and I
                    take full responsibility.

                    Tom:
                    Didn't this ever happen at
                    your last job?

    c) Joe slowly looks up.

                    Joe:
                    No. Oh, I guess I had a
                    few insulin reactions in
                    those years, but never at
                    work.

                    Tom:
                    And we never asked that you
                    have a driver's license ...

                    Joe:
                    No, see, then I couldn't
                    have taken the job ...

    d) Joe blinks his eyes, as if he might cry.

                    Joe:
                    You see why ... I could've
                    burned somebody ... or killed
                    them ...

    e) Joe puts his head in his hands.

                    I took a chance I didn't
                    have a right to take ...

                    (after a few seconds)

                    Tom:
                    Joe, how do you feel about
                    working with us?

"Decision-Making"

---

f) Joe raises his head.

                    Joe:
          I'd like to come back, very much.
          But I can't drive a fork lift.
          I probably can't pack ... not
          with hazardous chemicals around...

g) Joe lowers his head again, then lifts it and
tilts it toward Tom.

                    The worst part is that, as much
                    as I want to, I can't make
                    promises that I'll always
                    be okay.

dissolve to:

27. INT. TOM'S DESK AREA.

    Tom is sitting, pencil in hand, looking into
    space and thinking.

                              ANNOUNCER VOICE OVER:

                              IS IT TIME TO MAKE THE

                              DECISION? WHAT WOULD

                              YOU DO NOW?

cut to:

28. ARTWORK: DISCUSSION BREAK.

                              STOP THE TAPE AND TALK

                              ABOUT YOUR IDEAS AND

                              PLANS.

FADE OUT

FADE IN:

29. INT. OPERATIONS MANAGER'S OFFICE.

    Al is seated behind his desk and Tom walks in.
    He sits down and they talk, but we don't hear them.

                              ANNOUNCER VOICE OVER:

                              DECISIONS DON'T COME

                              EASY.

"Decision-Making"

ANNOUNCER VOICE OVER:

AND THERE ISN'T ALWAYS

A RIGHT OR WRONG

ANSWER. BUT THERE ARE

SOME STEPS YOU SHOULD

ALWAYS TAKE TO HELP

YOU MAKE A WISE

DECISION.

dissolve to:

A series of scenes; voice over only.

30. Replay from Scene 2: Hank, the other fork lift
    operator, is talking to Tom.

FIRST, GET ALL THE

FACTS.

dissolve to:

31. Replay from Scene 17. Packer #1 is remarking that
    Joe drank apple juice.

THEN, VERIFY THE FACTS.

dissolve to:

32. Replay from Scene 18. Tom looks at the
    computer printout sheets.

IDENTIFY THE REAL

PROBLEM.

dissolve to:

33. Replay from Scene 24. Tom talking to Al in
    his office.

CITE RESTRICTIONS ON A

SOLUTION.

"Decision-Making"

Page 19

dissolve to:

34. Replay from Scene 24. Al leaning over the desk
    toward Tom.

                    NAME SOME POSSIBLE

                    SOLUTIONS.

dissolve to:

35. Replay from Scene 26. Tom and Joe talk in the
    Coffee Shop.

                    TEST, OR DISCUSS, THESE

                    POSSIBLE SOLUTIONS.

dissolve to:

36. Replay from Scene 27. Tom sitting at desk,
    thinking.

                    FINALLY, MAKE THE

                    DECISION. ANY DECISION

                    SHOULD HAVE TWO

                    DISTINCT PARTS: AN

                    OVERALL DECISION.

                    AND, A SPECIFIC PLAN

                    OF ACTION.

dissolve to:

37. INT. HALLWAY.

    Tom and Joe walk toward the camera, talking.
    Hold on them until Joe fills the screen as he
    passes.

                    DECISION-MAKING IS,

                    PERHAPS, THE MOST

                    COMPLEX AND CRITICAL

                    PART OF ANY SUPERVISORS

                    JOB.

"Decision-Making"

<u>ANNOUNCER VOICE OVER</u>:

MAKE DECISIONS WITH

UNDERSTANDING,

WITH CAUTION,

AND WITH WISDOM.

<u>SUPER</u>: Company logo.

FADE OUT

SCRIPT
"The Truck Builders"

Donna Matrazzo
Scripts and Concepts

The Westbury #1101
271 South 15th Street
Philadelphia, PA 19102
(215) 545-2896

Freightliner Corporation

"THE TRUCK BUILDERS"

ROUGH SCRIPT

(Date)

"The Truck Builders"

VIDEOTAPE REQUIREMENTS

PURPOSE: To inform the viewer of the corporation's
scope through a presentation of its
history, products, organization,
manufacturing and philosophy.

To create a feeling that this a good company
to work for, and a company on the move.

To instill a sense of pride.

AUDIENCE: PRIMARY: New or prospective employees
(including campus recruitment).

SECONDARY: Current employees, dealers,
customers, financial groups, local and
civic organizations.

REQUESTED BY: (Client's name, number and location)

PRODUCER/DIRECTOR: (Name, number and location)

WRITER: (Name, number)

SCHEDULE:

Script Treatment: (Date)
Rough Script
Final Script:
Production Planning Meeting:
Shooting Dates:
Edit Date(s):
Final Presentation:
Distribution:

Shelf life of program: At least five years

"The Truck Builders"

```
                    "THE TRUCK BUILDERS"


FADE IN:
1. PHOTOGRAPHS/SLIDES
   A very fast-paced, exciting montage of sepia-tone and black/white
   old photographs or slides that give a sense of the times, and the
   company's beginnings. (Most of these are in your files.)  Match
   the cuts to the beats of the music.

                    MUSIC: Fast-paced, 1930's-style
                    with lots of plinking piano UP AND UNDER

                    SFX: Appropriate to visuals:
                    Horns honking, engines revving, etc.

Examples:
                              NARRATOR: (VOICE OVER)
-People by Model T's          (Deep, easy-going voice with just
-Old magazines                a hint of a drawl)
-"1929" in stylized type
-"Flapper" and others
 .at party                    IT'S 1929.

-Highway lined with Model T's
-Old construction scenes      AMERICA BEGINS THE BEST
-Men pouring cement
-Old "earthmover" digging     HIGHWAY SYSTEM IN THE WORLD.
  roadbed

-Leland James                 LELAND JAMES BEGINS THE BEST
-Old "Freight Terminal"
-Driver with "Consolidated    TRUCKING SYSTEM IN AMERICA:
  Truck Lines" truck
-Line-up of about fifty
  Consolidated trucks         CONSOLIDATED TRUCK LINES.

-Truck at dock
-Trucks on city street        YET, AFTER TEN YEARS,
-Trucks in warehouse
-Old magazine ad for truck    HE STILL HADN'T FOUND A TRUCK

                              TO MEET HIS DEMANDS.

                              SO, HE DESIGNED HIS OWN.


2. SLIDES
   To change pace, make all photographs in this section into slides.
   Project them and do camera moves on them, dissolving between them.
   SUPERIMPOSE engineering drafting designs over the truck scenes.
```

"The Truck Builders"

```
                                                              Page 2
                        MUSIC segues into a harder,
                        heavier, more rumbling kind of
                        sound UP AND UNDER

Examples:                       NARRATOR: (VOICE OVER)·

-The first cab-over truck       REVOLUTIONARY!
-Workers building the
    truck                       MADE OF ALUMINUM.

                                WITH A CAB-OVER-ENGINE DESIGN.
-Leland with new
    truck
-Different models of            CAN'T BE DONE,
    new truck
                                THE TRUCK BUILDERS SAID.

-Freightways crossing
    bridge                      SO JAMES BECAME A TRUCK BUILDER.
-Freightways in dust
    storm                       AND CALLED HIS A FREIGHTWAYS.

-Early manufacturing            A TON LIGHTER AND FOUR FEET
    scenes
-Freightways logo               SHORTER THAN ANYTHING ON THE ROAD.
    in ad

                                A MATCH FOR THE LONG, RUGGED
-Pan down long,
    rugged-looking highway      HIGHWAYS OF AMERICA.


3. PHOTOGRAPHS/SLIDES
   Again, to change pace, a series of quick-paced cuts -- beauty
   shots and old ads for the trucks.  During the sequence, the
   color changes from sepia tone to black/white to full color.

                        MUSIC segues into a lighter,
                        more rhythmic sound UP AND UNDER

a) Beauty shots of truck.       THE NAME CHANGED TO FREIGHTLINER.
   Close-up of logo on
   ads.                         AND THE CHANGES CONTINUED.
```

"The Truck Builders"

	NARRATOR: (VOICE OVER)
b) Sepia series	FREIGHTLINER INTRODUCED: (read with some rhythm)
-Integrated sleeper unit	THE SLEEPER ...
-Doubles -4-wheel drive	THE DOUBLES ...
	AND THE FOUR-WHEEL DRIVE.
c) Black/white series	
-Space Maker	THE SPACE-MAKER ...
-Dromedary -90-degree tilt cab	DROMEDARY ...
	AND THE 90-DEGREE TILT.
d) Full color series	
-Half cab	THE HALF-CAB ...
-Turboliner -Powerliner	TURBOLINER ... POWERLINER ...
-Conventional	AND THE CONVENTIONAL.
dissolve to: e) The Freightliner logo.	
	THE FREIGHTLINER.
dissolve to: f) Hyster #1 in the Smithsonian.	
	STANDING TODAY
	IN THE SMITHSONIAN.
	A LEGACY IN AMERICAN TRUCKING.

MUSIC UP AND OUT

Dip to black and up to:
4. EXT. HIGHWAY. DAY.
   The camera is set high (truck logo level) in the middle of the
   road. The truck is off in the distance, headed directly to the
   camera. It continues until its Freightliner logo is full screen.

"The Truck Builders"

MUSIC: A strong, hard-driving   Page 4
sound UP AND UNDER

SFX: Background sounds

(scene continues)

NARRATOR: (VOICE OVER)

FREIGHTLINER TODAY:

A COMPANY ON THE MOVE.

PART OF DAIMLER-BENZ ...

THE WORLD'S LARGEST

HEAVY-TRUCK PRODUCER.

A MULTI-MILLION DOLLAR CORPORATION

OF MASTER TRUCK BUILDERS.

CREATING THE BIGGEST

CUSTOM-DESIGNED TRUCKS ON THE ROAD:

DIESEL CLASS 8'S.

AND STILL, THE LEADER

IN QUALITY AND INNOVATION.

FREIGHTLINER ...

THE ROYALTY OF THE ROAD.

MUSIC CRESCENDO UP

5. LOGO MATTE/CORPORATE HEADQUARTERS BUILDING.
   From the close-up of the Freightliner logo, chroma-key an eye-level
   shot of the headquarters in Portland. Establish, then wipe off
   the truck framing the logo and replace it with a MATTE. Inside
   the matte, continue with a series of cuts and scenes of people
   working at their desks in offices -- from open work areas to
   cubicles to executives in a conference room.

                    MUSIC segues into a lighter version
                    of the same piece UP AND UNDER

"The Truck Builders"

<u>MUSIC</u> <u>UNDER</u>   Page 5

                              <u>NARRATOR</u>: (VOICE OVER)

                              TODAY, FREIGHTLINER IS <u>PEOPLE</u>.

                              PEOPLE IN <u>OFFICES</u>.

                              PROFESSIONAL MEN AND WOMEN

                              WHO DESIGN, FINANCE AND

                              MARKET TRUCKS.

6. LOGO MATTE/PARTS AND TRUCK PLANTS
   Wipe left to right across the scene in the matte to reveal the
   interior of a manufacturing plant. Continue with a series of
   scenes of people working in both parts and truck plants -- at
   machines and on the assembly lines.

                              FREIGHTLINER IS PEOPLE <u>IN</u> <u>PLANTS</u>.

                              MASTER WORKERS WHO TAKE ON

                              THE CHALLENGE OF BUILDING

                              COMPLEX, CUSTOM TRUCKS.

7. LOGO MATTE/PARTS DISTRIBUTION CENTER
   Wipe right to left to reveal the interior of a parts distribution
   center. Continue with a series of scenes of people typing at
   CRT terminals, driving motorized picking machines down warehouse
   aisles and packing parts to be shipped.

                              FREIGHTLINER IS PEOPLE

                              IN <u>PARTS</u> <u>DISTRIBUTION</u> <u>CENTERS</u>.

                              USING THE MOST SOPHISTICATED

                              COMPUTER NETWORK IN THE

                              TRUCKING INDUSTRY.

8. LOGO MATTE/DEALERSHIP
   Wipe left to right to reveal the exterior of a dealership.
   Continue with a series of scenes of a dealer showing a
   Freightliner to one customer, a Mercedes-Benz truck to another.

"The Truck Builders"

NARRATOR: (VOICE OVER)

AND, FREIGHTLINER IS PEOPLE

IN DEALERSHIPS.

SPECIALLY-PICKED DEALERS WHO

SELL FREIGHTLINER AND MERCEDES-BENZ

TRUCKS FROM COAST TO COAST.

9. LOGO MATTE/FACILITY EXTERIORS
a) Wipe right to left to reveal people leaving a plant at the
   end of a shift. Continue with a series of scenes of people
   leaving headquarters in Portland and other facilities.

FREIGHTLINER IS PEOPLE:

GROWING IN A GROWING COMPANY.

FACED WITH CHALLENGES,

RESPONSIBILITIES,

AND A CHANCE TO DEVELOP.

b) One person, wearing a Freightliner jacket, walks toward the
   camera until the Freightliner logo fills the logo space in the
   matte.

FREIGHTLINER PEOPLE ...

EVERY ONE, A TRUCK BUILDER.

MUSIC UP AND OUT

Dip to black and up to:
10. INT. STUDIO OR OPEN AREA OF MANUFACTURING PLANT SET UP WITH
    BLACK PAPER ROLLS.
a) Black background. Slowly dissolve on (or suddenly light with a
   series of spotlights) beauty shots of two trucks (COE AND
   Conventional). Use star filter to make chrome glimmer.

MUSIC: Classical-style, drum-heavy,
"2001"-sounding UP AND UNDER

"The Truck Builders"

```
                    MUSIC UNDER                              Page 7

                              NARRATOR: (VOICE OVER)

                              FREIGHTLINERS ...

                              THE ULTIMATE TRUCKS.

  b) Continue with a series of slow dissolves -- panning up, down
     and around the two trucks.  Alternate chrome and glassy
     parts with matte finish parts.  Show detailed parts and
     painting on truck.

  c) Alternate these slow, graceful shots with a few quick cutaways
     of sophisticated engineering techniques which brought the
     machines into existence.

  Examples:
  -    The computer terminal with a display of truck
       "mode shake" vibrations.
  -    A close-up of an oscilloscope.
  -    Full-scale drafting layout on the 18-foot lofting board.
  -    Truck on 25,000-lb. "torture" hydraulic jack.
  -    Noise analysis lines on computer display.

       Give all of these scenes a visual elegance.  End with a
       zoom-in to the glittery chrome and go out of focus.

                              (over entire sequence)


                              CUSTOM BUILT.

                              FROM THE ROAD UP.

                              BEAUTIFUL.  RUGGED.  EFFICIENT.

                              ENGINEERED FOR EXCELLENCE.


                              THE FREIGHTLINER CONVENTIONAL:

                              WHEN POWER COUNTS,

                              IT GIVES THE MOST.


                              AND, THE CAB-OVER-ENGINE, OR C-O-E

                              WHEN INCHES COUNT, IT TAKES THE

                              LEAST.
```

"The Truck Builders"

                            MUSIC UNDER   Page 8

                                        NARRATOR: (VOICE OVER, continuing)

(continue montage)   BUILT FOR COMFORT,

                                        EFFICIENCY, RELIABILITY.

                                        THE MILLION-MILE MACHINE.

                                        CREATED WITH STATE-OF-THE-ART

                                        EXPERTISE.

                                        FREIGHTLINER TRUCKS:

                                        THE ULTIMATE IN WORKMANSHIP.

                                        THE ULTIMATE IN OWNERSHIP.

                            MUSIC UP AND OUT

Dip to black and up to:
11. INT. DEALER FACILITY. OFFICE AREA.
 a) A close-up on TSO (Truck Sales Order) Work Sheet. Pull back to
    see CUSTOMER-HANK (wearing plaid flannel shirt and jeans) and
    DEALER-DENNIS (wearing shirt and tie).

 b) Cut back and forth as they talk and the Dealer fills in the
    information on the sheets. (Show that there are 3-4 pages
    of specs).

                            SFX: Background sounds UNDER
                            VOICES of the two men UNDER

                                        TO A DRIVER, A TRUCK IS MORE

                                        THAN A VEHICLE.

                                        IT'S HIS BUSINESS,

                                        HIS CAPITAL INVESTMENT,

                                        HIS HOME-ON-THE-ROAD.

                                        IT'S HIS LIFE.

                                        SO EVERY DETAIL IS IMPORTANT.

"The Truck Builders"

```
BACKGROUND SOUNDS UNDER          Page 9
SYNC VOICES UP

HANK: (Lip Sync)

Y'know, I really like that
conventional, but I'm gonna be
hauling the maximum load ... and
I'm not sure it could make
the legal weight transfer.

DENNIS:

No problem.  With your specs,
we can set it up with a 240-inch
wheel base ... locate the fuel tanks ...
VOICES UNDER

                 NARRATOR: (VOICE OVER)

                 EVERY FREIGHTLINER STARTS WITH

                 A CUSTOMER AND A DEALER.

                 THE CUSTOMER KNOWS HIS JOB.

                 AND THE DEALER KNOWS WHAT OPTIONS

                 WILL GET THE JOB DONE.

VOICES UP
DENNIS:

... an engine in the 400-horsepower
range rated at 2100 rpm's.

HANK:

What kind of fuel economy's
that gonna give me?
VOICES UNDER


b) Dennis turns a notebook around for Hank to see and points to
   some figures.

                 THERE'S NO SUCH THING

                 AS A STANDARD MODEL.
```

"The Truck Builders"

NARRATOR: (VOICE OVER)

EVERY FREIGHTLINER IS

CUSTOM-DESIGNED ... INCH FOR INCH..

BY THE PERSON WHO WILL DRIVE IT ...

MILE AFTER MILE.

dissolve to:
 c) Over the shoulder shot as the Dealer, alone at his desk, looks
    over the TSO. Zoom in as he signs it and seals it in an
    envelope addressed to Freightliner Sales Office in Portland.

SFX: Continue to pick up background
sounds through Scene 21 UNDER

EVERY ORDER IS SENT ...

match dissolve to:
12. INT. CORPORATE HEADQUARTERS. SALES COORDINATION DEPARTMENT.
    A close-up of the envelope being opened. Pull back to a
    medium shot of SALES COORDINATOR at desk. He/she takes out
    order and gives it a Serial Number (#25000).

... THROUGH THE SALES OFFICE

IN PORTLAND.

dissolve to:
13. INT. CORPORATE HEADQUARTERS. SALES COMMUNICATION DEPT.
    A close-up of the computer terminal screen, with #25000
    plainly visible. Pan around to see COMPUTER OPERATOR typing
    numbers from the TSO into the computer.

SPECIALISTS ANALYZE THE ORDER.

AND FEED THE SPECS

INTO THE COMPUTER.

dissolve to:
14. INT. CORPORATE HEADQUARTERS. CUSTOM ENGINEERING DEPT.
    Over the shoulder shot of SPEC WRITER looking through 3-4 page
    printout, then turning to large encyclopedia-like book, checking
    one of the numbers.

"The Truck Builders"

```
                    BACKGROUND SOUNDS UNDER          Page 11

                                 NARRATOR: (VOICE OVER)

                                 FROM THE COMPUTER PRINTOUT,

                                 THAT TRUCK IS BUILT ON PAPER.

                                 BY SPEC WRITERS ...

cut to: (or pan around - they sit at angles from each other)
15. SAME AREA.
    Over the shoulder shot of FRAME CHARTER rearranging different
    colors of plastic overlays over a drawing of an axle.

                                 ... AND FRAME CHARTERS.

                                 WHO MAKE SURE ALL SPECS

                                 ARE COMPATIBLE.

dissolve to:
16. INT. CORPORATE HEADQUARTERS. CUSTOM ENGINEERING.
    A dolly shot down the aisle past the DRAFTSMEN, working at
    drawing boards.

                                 THOSE THAT ARE NOT,

                                 ARE RE-WORKED BY CUSTOM

                                 ENGINEERS.

dissolve to:
17. INT. CORPORATE HEADQUARTERS. SALES COMMUNICATION DEPT.
    A COMPUTER OPERATOR types new specs into the computer
    terminal.
                                 THIS INFORMATION IS FED

                                 BACK INTO THE COMPUTER ...

dissolve to:
18. INT. CORPORATE HEADQUARTERS. COMPUTER ROOM.
    Series of dissolves around Computer Room to give the feeling
    of much action and sophistication:  Reels spinning, buttons
    lighting up in a sequence, screens lighting up with data,
    disc doors opening automatically, and so forth.

                                 THE BIGGEST AND MOST

                                 SOPHISTICATED COMPUTER SYSTEM

                                 IN THE TRUCKING BUSINESS.
```

"The Truck Builders"

BACKGROUND SOUNDS UNDER

NARRATOR: (VOICE OVER)

IT COORDINATES ENGINEERING

SPECS WITH PLANT SCHEDULES,

INVENTORY, DELIVERIES,

AND SPECIAL REQUESTS.

dissolve to:
19. SAME LOCATION OR STAGED ANYWHERE.
    A close-up of readout on screen or printout coming off
    printer.

IT TELLS WHEN AND WHERE

THE TRUCK WILL BE BUILT ...

match dissolve to:
20. INT. TRUCK MANUFACTURING PLANT. COMPUTER AREA.
  a) Close-up on printout as it comes off printer. Pull back
     to see PERSON (wearing workman's matching pant/shirt)
     tear off printout. Pull back to establish that this is a
     truck manufacturing plant.

... AND THEN,

IT TELLS THE TRUCK PLANT.

cut to:
  b) Close-up of printout to see #25000.

SFX: Telephone dialing
(sound from next scene)

dissolve to:
21. INT. DEALER FACILITY. OFFICE AREA.
    Dealer talking on phone to customer, reading from paper.

DENNIS: (Lip Sync, on phone)

Hi, Hank. This is Dennis.
I just got word that your
truck'll be ready for delivery
the morning of June 6th. (pause)
Okay, see you then, Hank.

"The Truck Builders"

dissolve to:
22. INT. PARTS MANUFACTURING PLANT.
    Series of cuts and/or dissolves emphasizing two things:
    detailed quality of parts, and skills of people. Shoot
    from behind, under and around equipment. Make it look
    sophisticated, but scenes should look as though people
    are in control.

Examples:
- MACHINE SHOP. Shooting from floor, medium shot of
  NC WORKER at controls of NC machine.
- MACHINE SHOP. Side angle of CRAFTSMAN at saw, carefully
  cutting pipe.
- PAINT AREA. PAINTER in white suit and mask, spray-painting
  parts.
- TOOL/DIE AREA. PRESS OPERATOR at press, stamping out
  part, taking it off mold and inspecting it.
- WELDING AREA. WELDER, spot welding.
- MACHINE SHOP. WORKER moving grille across huge stamping
  machine.
- QA STAMPING AREA. PERSON performing Quality Assurance test.
- MACHINE SHOP. Close-up of MAN'S HAND measuring bolt with
  small gauge.

                    SFX: Background sounds UNDER

                    MUSIC: Lively, fast-paced
                    sound UP AND UNDER

                            NARRATOR: (VOICE OVER)
                            (over entire sequence)

                            QUALITY BEGINS

                            WITH PARTS MANUFACTURING.

                            BECAUSE A TRUCK ...

                            ESPECIALLY A CUSTOM TRUCK ...

                            IS ONLY AS GOOD AS ITS PARTS.

                            AND THE PEOPLE WHO MAKE THEM.

"The Truck Builders"

MUSIC/BACKGROUND SOUNDS UNDER

NARRATOR: (VOICE OVER)

AT FREIGHTLINER,

QUALITY IS AN ATTITUDE.

EACH PERSON IS WORKING TO MAKE

EVERY PART ... PERFECT.

sequence ends with:
23. INT. PARTS MANUFACTURING PLANT. SHIPPING AREA.
    PACKER is putting chrome part in shipping box. Zoom in to
    see "Freightliner Parts" on box.

THEIRS IS A SENSE OF PRIDE.

BECAUSE THEY'RE BUILDING MORE

THAN A TRUCK OR ITS PARTS.

THEY'RE BUILDING

THE FREIGHTLINER NAME.

match dissolve to:
24. INT. TRUCK MANUFACTURING PLANT. RECEIVING AREA.
    A close-up of the "Freightliner Parts" on the box. Pull back
    to see a RECEIVER take the part out of its box and check the
    number with specs on printout for #25000.

THE PARTS ... BECOME ...

THE MACHINE.

dissolve to:
25. INT. TRUCK MANUFACTURING PLANT. ASSEMBLY LINES.
    Series of dissolves to give the impression that #25000 is being
    built -- from skeleton to finished truck. Duplicate the kind
    of marking used in the plant for #25000 and put it on every
    "truck" shot. Try to get ONE or TWO PEOPLE in each shot.

Possible sequence:
-   CAB. With engine tunnel, roof bows and deck plates.
-   CHASSIS. WORKERS on assembly line with frame rails and cross
    members.
-   CAB. With back and roof skins and doors.
-   CHASSIS. With air lines, wiring and air tanks.
-   CAB. Marked for painting.

"The Truck Builders"

MUSIC/BACKGROUND SOUNDS UNDER

- CHASSIS. With engine and radiator.
- CAB. Being spray-painted.
- CAB. With door open, seats installed.
- CHASSIS. Painted cab is being led by a hoist onto the frame.
- QC AREA. PERSON checking finished cab using gauges.
- QC AREA. Full shot of finished truck.

MUSIC segues into a heavier-sounding piece UP AND UNDER

NARRATOR: (VOICE OVER)

IT TAKES TWO ASSEMBLY

LINES:

THE CAB, AND THE CHASSIS.

THE CAB NEEDS TWO DAYS MORE,

SO IT'S BEGUN FIRST.

ALONG THE LINE

ARE PARTS AND PEOPLE.

CRUCIAL PARTS ... FROM

BUMPER TO TAIL LIGHTS ...

THAT MAKE EACH TRUCK

A STANDARD OF EXCELLENCE.

AND CRUCIAL PEOPLE ...

ABLE TO HANDLE SUCH COMPLEX

AND CRITICAL ASSEMBLY.

WHERE EVERY PART

MUST BE THE RIGHT PART.

"The Truck Builders"

MUSIC/BACKGROUND SOUNDS UNDER

(continue sequence)

> NARRATOR: (VOICE OVER, continuing)
>
> AND MUST FIT,
>
> TO THE FRACTION OF AN INCH.
>
> PEOPLE, PARTS AND SCHEDULES ...
>
> IN PERFECT SYNCHRONIZATION.
>
> THUS, THE TRUCK IS BUILT.
>
> AND THEN, INTENSIVELY CHECKED.

dissolve to:
26. INT/EXT. DOORWAY.
    The truck is framed in the doorway, facing outside. See #25000.
    The truck drives toward the camera.

> SFX: Truck engine starting
>
> NOW, THIS FREIGHTLINER IS READY
>
> TO MEET ITS DESIGNER.

Dip to black and up to:
27. EXT. DEALER FACILITY.
    Truck #25000 is parked in front of the dealership. Hank and
    Dennis walk around to the front. Follow with camera as Hank
    walks closely around the truck, cups his hand above his eyes
    and looks up at it, and rubs his hand over the paint design.
    He breaks into a grin and Dennis hands him the keys. He climbs up

> MUSIC segues into a lively
> sound UP

cut to:
28. INT. CAB OF TRUCK.
    Hank sits behind the wheel, leans back, wrapping fingers tightly
    around steering wheel. He looks at the knobs and controls and
    twists, presses and pulls a few different ones.

    He looks at the seat beside him. With one hand he spreads out
    the books there to look at them -- Warranty books, Drivers
    Manual, Maintenance books.

    He looks down over the steering wheel at Dennis and signals him
    to join him. A close-up as he flips the keys in his hand, holds
    them to look at them, then turns the key in the ignition.

"The Truck Builders"

```
                              SFX: Key in ignition, engine
                              starting
cut to:
29. EXT. DEALER FACILITY.
    Shoot from ground and see Hank and Dennis in cab. (Should
    be angled so Hank truly looks like "King of the Road".)
    The truck drives past the camera.  End as the spinning
    wheel drives past the screen. (the screen is dark.)


                      MUSIC/BACKGROUND SOUNDS UP AND OUT
dissolve to:
30. PHOTOGRAPHS/MATTE FOR FOUR PHOTOS.
    A black matte.  Beginning upper left, then lower right,
    lower left, then upper right: Pop on and continually
    change (in same order) slides or backlit negatives of:

-   Freightliner dealership exteriors
-   Dealership interiors
-   Medium and close-up shots of dealers
-   Mercedes-Benz dealership exteriors
-   M-B dealership interiors
-   Dealers' multicolored notebooks
-   Dealers' Service Departments
-   Mechanics
    FINAL STILL:  A dealer is typing on his red computer
    terminal.  Zoom in to make this shot full screen, then
    continue to zoom in to the readout.


                          MUSIC: With a strong beat so
                          pop-ons can be cut to its rhythm
                          UP AND UNDER

                                    NARRATOR: (VOICE OVER)

                                    INDEPENDENT DEALERS

                                    FROM COAST TO COAST

                                    SELL FREIGHTLINERS AND

                                    MERCEDES-BENZ.


                                    CUSTOMERS ... AND ALL

                                    FREIGHTLINER PEOPLE ...

                                    COUNT ON THE DEALERS.
```

"The Truck Builders"

MUSIC UNDER

NARRATOR: (VOICE OVER)

TO SELL THE TRUCKS.

AND TO SERVICE THEM.

match dissolve to:
31. INT. DEALER FACILITY. (LIVE ACTION)
    A close-up of the display -- a request for parts.

dissolve to:
32. EXT. HIGHWAY.
    a) Truck stopped on side of road. (Not #25000)

GETTING A TRUCK ON THE ROAD

IS A TOUGH JOB.

SO IS KEEPING IT THERE.

b) Cab tilted; DRIVER looking under hood.

SERVICE CAN'T BE JUST GOOD.

IT'S GOT TO BE GREAT.

dissolve to:
33. INT. WAREHOUSE.
    A WORKER takes a part from a shelf.

SERVICE MEANS PARTS.

AVAILABLE WHEN THEY'RE NEEDED.

WHERE THEY'RE NEEDED.

cut to:
34. INT. WAREHOUSE. OFFICE AREA.
    a) PERSON is seated at terminal beneath a Parts Express logo. He
    picks up the phone and dials.

SO, FREIGHTLINER HAS:

THE PARTS EXPRESS.

THE BEST SUPPLY SYSTEM

IN THE BUSINESS.

b) Pan up to MAP with dealer locations HIGHLIGHTED.

"The Truck Builders"

```
                    MUSIC UNDER                        Page 19

                              NARRATOR: (VOICE OVER)

                              140,000 PARTS AVAILABLE

                              TO EACH DEALER ...

  c) Add HIGHLIGHTED LINES leading to Distribution Centers.

                                   ... WITH AN UP-TO-THE-SECOND

                              COMPUTER LINE TO

                              NEARBY DISTRIBUTION CENTERS.

cut back to:
35. INT. DEALER FACILITY (SAME AS SCENE 31)
    Dealer turns around.  Pull back to see MECHANIC wiping hands
    with rag and talking to driver.

                              SERVICE A DRIVER

                              CAN COUNT ON.

                              BECAUSE HE HAS TO.


                    MUSIC UP AND OUT
dissolve to:
36. EXT. CORPORATE HEADQUARTERS.
    A beauty shot of the building.

                         MUSIC: A light, low key sound
                         UP AND UNDER

                              AT CORPORATE HEADQUARTERS,

                              FREIGHTLINER PEOPLE BUILD TRUCKS

                              IN A LOT OF DIFFERENT WAYS:
cut to:
37. ACCOUNTING DEPT.
    PEOPLE IN ACCOUNTING, looking over computer printout sheets.

                              THEY ANALYZE COSTS,

                              AND BUILD TRUCKS IN DOLLARS.
cut to:
38. ENGINEERING DEPT.
    An ENGINEER works at a computer terminal; a truck in various
    configurations appears on the screen.
```

"The Truck Builders"

NARRATOR: (VOICE OVER)

THEY BUILD TRUCKS ON COMPUTERS:

DESIGNING NEW STYLES AND

IMPROVING OLD ONES.

cut to:
39. MARKETING DEPT.
    Over the shoulder shot of MARKETING PEOPLE looking at ads
    and brochures laid out on table.

THEY ANALYZE THE MARKET

AND THEY BUILD THE

FREIGHTLINER IMAGE.

cut to:
40. TECHNICAL PUBLICATIONS DEPT.
    WRITERS looking over key art for a manual, with line drawings
    of truck.

THEY BUILD TRUCKS IN INK ...

cut to:
41. EXT. CORPORATE HEADQUARTERS.
    PHOTOGRAPHER taking photo of truck.

... AND ON FILM.

cut to:
42. INT. SMALL CONFERENCE ROOM.
    PERSON watching slide show -- assembly line sequence of
    "Building the Efficient Machine".

AND, FREIGHTLINER PEOPLE

BUILD TRUCKS IN TRAINING PROGRAMS

FOR MECHANICS ...

cut to:
43. INT. LARGE CLASSROOM.
    MECHANIC in work uniform is drawing on a blackboard in front of
    a classroom of people.

... DEALERS, AND EMPLOYEES.

cut to:
44. CORPORATE HEADQUARTERS
    Series of cuts of a few pieces of "Freightliner" art. Examples:
    -   INT. 2nd Floor. EXECUTIVE WAITING AREA. Watercolor of truck.
    -   INT. EXECUTIVE OFFICE AREA. Fabric print of truck.
    -   EXT. FRONT ENTRANCE. Red "logo" sculpture.
    -   INT. OFFICE. Replica model of truck on desk.

"The Truck Builders"

```
              MUSIC UNDER                          Page 21

                              NARRATOR: (VOICE OVER)

                              CUSTOM WORK.  AND CUSTOM

                              PROGRAMS.

                              DONE BY AND FOR

                              FREIGHTLINER PEOPLE.

                              THE CUSTOM TRUCK BUILDERS.
"match" dissolve to:
45. EXT. HIGHWAY(S).
      Series of cuts of different kinds of Freightliners on the road.
      Take from different angles as they whoosh past camera.  Alternate
      left to right, from bridge to see payload, and so forth.


Examples:
-    Produce/steel hauler/chemical/bottlers
-    New cars/refrigeration/cargo containers
-    Lumber/construction, and so forth

                              MUSIC: Country-western style, lots
                              of banjo/fiddle UP AND UNDER

                              SFX:  Background sounds UNDER

                                        FREIGHTLINERS ARE EVERYWHERE.

                                        BRINGING THE THINGS

                                        AMERICANS WANT AND NEED ...

                                        RIGHT TO THEM.

                              MUSIC/SOUNDS UP


Dip to black and up to:
46. ART/PHOTOGRAPHS.
      SLOW WIPE FROM UPPER LEFT TO LOWER RIGHT:
   a) Large piece of art with 30-40 photos.  (Either all close-ups
      of Freightliner people or those alternated with different
      trucks.)

                              MUSIC segues to light,
                              low-key sound UP AND UNDER

                                        FREIGHTLINER PEOPLE:

                                        FIRST, THEY SEEMED COURAGEOUS.
```

"The Truck Builders"

MUSIC UNDER

NARRATOR: (VOICE OVER)

BUILDING THAT TRUCK

NO ONE ELSE WOULD DARE.

b) Another large piece of art. Repeat wipe.

THEN, THEY SEEMED PROUD.

BUILDING THAT TRUCK

EVERYONE ELSE WOULD COPY.

c) Another large piece of art -- this time, with chrome Freightliner
logo in center.

NOW, THEY SEEM WISE.

BUILDING THAT TRUCK FOR EFFICIENCY.

WHEN EFFICIENCY'S TIME HAS COME.

d) Wipe off last series of photos, keeping logo. Shine spotlights
and use star filter to make logo glimmer. SUPER Title "THE
TRUCK BUILDERS" on screen bottom.

FREIGHTLINER.

THE TRUCK BUILDERS.

FOR TODAY. AND TOMORROW.

e) The Title rolls up, behind the logo.

CREDITS FOLLOW

FADE OUT

RESOURCES

AMERICAN SOCIETY FOR TRAINING AND
DEVELOPMENT (ASTD)
600 Maryland Ave., SW
Suite 305
Washington, DC 20024

ASSOCIATION FOR EDUCATIONAL COMMUNICATIONS
& TECHNOLOGY (AECT)
1126 Sixteenth St., NW
Washington, DC 20036

ASSOCIATION FOR MULTI-IMAGE (AMI)
8019 N. Himes Ave.
Suite 401
Tampa, FL 33614

HEALTH EDUCATION MEDIA ASSOCIATION (HEMA)
PO Box 771
Riverdale, GA 30274

HEALTH SCIENCES COMMUNICATIONS ASSOCIATION
(HESCA)
Route 5, Box 311F
Midlothian, VA 23113

INFORMATION FILM PRODUCERS OF AMERICA (IFPA)
900 Palm Ave.
Suite B
Pasadena, CA 91030

INTERNATIONAL ASSOCIATION OF BUSINESS
COMMUNICATORS (IABC)
870 Market St.
Suite 940
San Francisco, CA 94102

INTERNATIONAL TELEVISION ASSOCIATION (ITVA)
6311 N. O'Connor Rd. #110
Irving, TX 75039

SOCIETY FOR TECHNICAL COMMUNICATION (STC)
815 Fifteenth St., NW
Washington, DC 20005

WRITERS GUILD OF AMERICA (WGA)
   East   West
      555 W. 57th St.   8955 Beverly Blvd.
      New York, NY 10019   Los Angeles, CA 90048

INDEX

FOR MORE INFORMATION

Books on business communications from Communicom Publishing Company

THE CORPORATE SCRIPTWRITING BOOK: A Step-by-Step Guide to Writing Business Films, Videotapes and Slide Shows, by Donna Matrazzo. Detailed techniques for creating exciting and effective audio visual scripts. Recommended for writers, producers, directors and managers.
210 pages   **$14.95**

THE VIDEO PRODUCTION GUIDE, by Lon McQuillin. A thorough guide to every facet of video production, from pre-production planning to direction techniques, single and multi-camera studio and location production, editing, special effects and distribution.
352 pages   **$28.95**

ORGANIZATIONAL TV NEWS, by Tom Thompson, award-winning producer of the longest-running employee TV News program in the country. A handbook of theory and production tips and techniques. Covers everything from looking for news stories to editing the final production.
217 pages   **$16.95**

EDITING YOUR NEWSLETTER: A Guide to Writing, Designing and Production, by Mark Beach. Shows how to raise newsletter quality and cut costs through improved writing, graphics, photography, formats, paste-up and printing.
128 pages   **$9.95**

THE SCRIPT READERS KIT: A Job Aid for Media Productions. A unique kit to simplify and save time with the complex process of script approvals. Separate guides for content specialist, executive, training designer, producer, director tell these people what to look for and how to "read" the script to make appropriate revisions.   **$19.95**

THE HANDBOOK OF PRIVATE TELEVISION, edited by Nathan Sambul. A comprehensive treatment from 27 well-known experts covers everything from selling concept to management, to installing, staffing and managing a video facility or network. Emphasizes sound management techniques and creative production approaches.
400 pages   **$74.95**

WRITE FOR FREE
DESCRIPTIVE BROCHURE

ORDER FORM

COMMUNICOM

548 N.E. 43rd Avenue, Portland, Oregon 97213 · (503) 239-5141

Please send me the following:

———— Copies of THE CORPORATE SCRIPTWRITING BOOK @ $14.95

———— Copies of THE VIDEO PRODUCTION GUIDE   @ $28.95

———— Copies of ORGANIZATIONAL TV NEWS   @ $16.95

———— Copies of EDITING YOUR NEWSLETTER   @ $ 9.95

———— Copies of THE SCRIPT READERS KIT   @ $19.95

———— Copies of HANDBOOK OF PRIVATE TELEVISION   @ $74.95

NAME ————————————————————————————

ORGANIZATION ————————————————————————

ADDRESS ————————————————————————————

————————————————————————————

Shipping: Please add $1.50 for the first book and $1.00 for each additional book.